The
Chesapeake Bay
Crab Cookbook

The Chesapeake Bay Crab Cookbook

John Shields
Photography by Jed Kirschbaum

Aris Books

Addison-Wesley Publishing Company, Inc.

Reading, Massachusetts   Menlo Park, California   New York
Don Mills, Ontario   Wokingham, England   Amsterdam   Bonn
Sydney   Singapore   Tokyo   Madrid   San Juan
Paris   Seoul   Milan   Mexico City   Taipei

Library of Congress Cataloging-in-Publication Data

Shields, John, (John Edward)
    The Chesapeake Bay crab cookbook / John Shields ; photography by
Jed Kirschbaum.
        p.   cm.
    ''Aris books.''
    ISBN 0-201-56762-8
    1. Cookery (Crabs)   2. Crabs—Chesapeake Bay Region (Md. and Va.)
I. Title.
    TX754.C83S55   1992
    641.6'95—dc20   91-38120
                                                          CIP

Cover design by Christine Leonard Raquepaw
Cover photography by Jed Kirschbaum
Text design by Janis Owens
Interior photography by Jed Kirschbaum
Technical illustrations by Pamela Manley
Illustrated map by Deborah Young
Set in 10-point Berkeley Old Style by Shepard Poorman
Communications Corporation

1 2 3 4 5 6 7 8 9-VB-95949392
First printing, March 1992

This book is dedicated with love to Mom-Mom
for bringing me to the Chesapeake, and to John Kelly
for giving me the distance.

It is also dedicated to the memory of two Chesapeake
cooking companions and longtime friends:
John Leisenring, who started me on my culinary career
by breaking his ankle, and to Sam Farace, lover of good
food, fine wine, and la vie.

· Contents ·

• Acknowledgments •

A bushel basket of crabs fresh off of Joe Businsky's boat,
The Jane B, at Benvy's Point makes its way to market.

One might not believe putting a little crab cookbook together could involve the help and support of so many, but in my case it sure did. I would like to express my thanks to all of the people who provided me with the recipes and family stories that made this book come to life.

For the logistics of making this book happen, many thanks to my agent Susan Lescher and to the wonderfully supportive and talented group at Aris/Addison-Wesley Publishing: John Harris, who got this whole project started; Greg Kaplan; Elizabeth Carduff; Robert Shepard; George Gibson; Gilly Hailparn; and Beth Burleigh; and to the world's best copy editor, Sharon Silva.

Muchas gracias to my Chesapeake crew: My family, including Mom-Mom, Lynnie, Patricia, Patrick, Kath, TJ, Kara, Tommy, and Joey, who all put up with me; Jed Kirschbaum, for his incredible photographs, brilliant concepts, and friendship; William Taylor; Tony (my PR man) Sartori and his family; the Chagoris family; Debra Botterill of McCormick Spice; the teachers and students of Kingsville Elementary School; Allan de la Reese and his English classes at Parkville Senior High; Katrina for the wheels; Mike and Betsy Delea for the crab-cracking outerwear; Ed Gunning, Calvin, and the staff at Gunning's Crab House for all of their help and cooperation; Mr. Leroy Hale, who knows almost more about blue crabs than any man alive; Nelda Di Lauro of Handy's Crabs; my girlfriends, Bonnie North, Sue Lowe, Di-Di Krause, Miss Myrna Thompson, Norina, and, oh my Gawd, lest I forget and be struck by lightning, Ms. Bertie Lou Reese, who is my recipe testing assistant and talented food demo setup gal.

I am very grateful to Chris White, who spent time talking and sharing his Bay knowledge with me on Tilghman Island, and to the staff at The Chesapeake Bay Foundation.

Over on the West Coast I need to express my gratitude to Linda Gerson for her editing expertise and moral support; John Kelly, my Gertie's cofounder and best friend; Mrs. DeLune and Maria-Maria for helping me avert various crab-overload nervous breakdowns, and, lastly, to Mr. TG Fraser, a whiz on the processing keys.

To these folks and any others who gave a hand along the way, many thanks and much love.

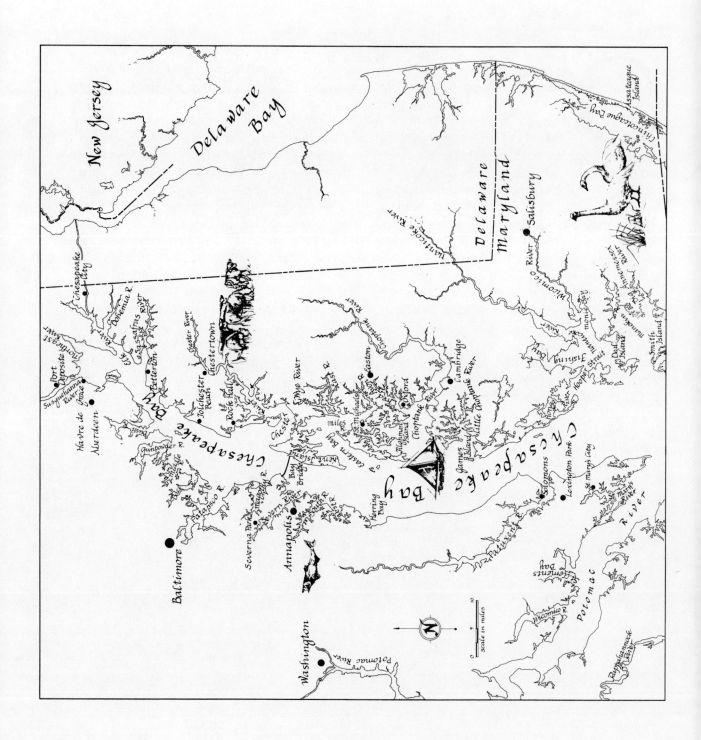

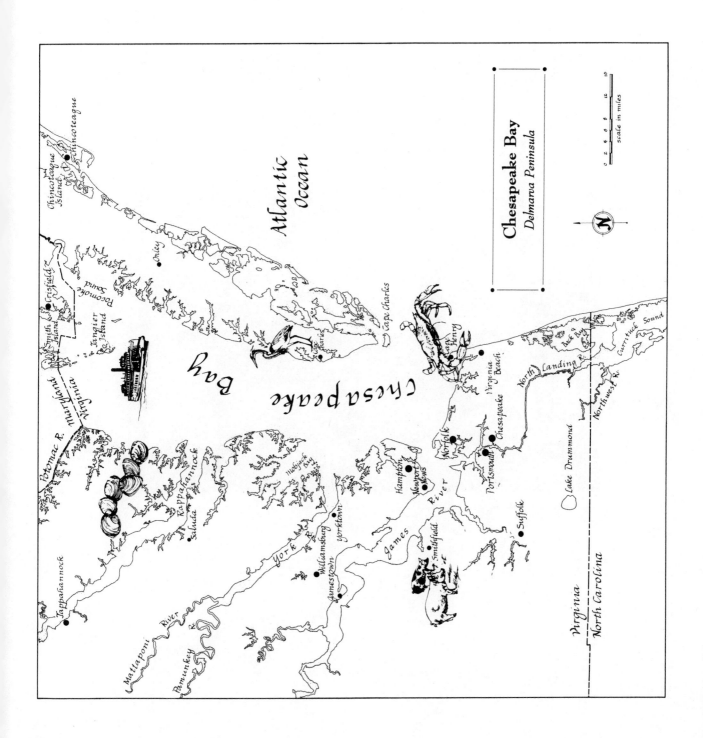

Chesapeake Bay
Delmarva Peninsula

scale in miles
0 2 4 6 8 10

N

Atlantic Ocean

Chesapeake Bay

Chincoteague

Chincoteague Island

Onley

Crisfield

Pocomoke Sound

Smith Island

Tangier Island

Maryland

Virginia

Potomac R.

Cape Charles

Cape Henry

Virginia Beach

Chesapeake Beach

Back Bay

Currituck Sound

North Landing R.

Northwest R.

Norfolk

Portsmouth

Hampton

Newport News

Suffolk

Lake Drummond

Virginia

North Carolina

Mobjack Bay

Rappahannock

Saluda

Tappahannock

York River

Mattaponi River

Pamunkey R.

Williamsburg

Jamestown

Yorktown

James

River

Smithfield

• The Chesapeake's Beautiful Swimmers •

*A calm autumn sunrise finds workboats on Crab Alley Creek
at Kent Island, Maryland.*

More cooking from the Chesapeake Bay? You'd better believe it . . . and now we're talking crabs. Blue crabs, that is. And better eating is hard to find.

It seems like only yesterday that I started my odyssey through the homes, kitchens, farms, workboats, and marketplaces along the Chesapeake Bay. The result of those wanderings was *The Chesapeake Bay Cookbook*, a culinary *Amarcord* of my homeland. I discovered an array of delicious recipes, a treasure chest of family tales and lore, and a cast of characters from the towns and cities of the Chesapeake. Not only was I made privy to recipes that had been handed down from one generation to the next, but I met and befriended some of the most remarkable people I have ever been privileged to know.

Compiling the information and writing the book was one of the most exhilarating and rewarding experiences of my life. I felt it was immensely important to record the Chesapeake food experience not only for the rest of the world, but also so that we peoples of the Chesapeake could reaffirm our culinary heritage and our pride in the gifts we receive from the magnificent body of water that so shapes our lives. Judging from my mail and the many people I've spoken with on both sides of the Chesapeake, that pride is reasserting itself. Folks are taking a new look at what they have right in their own backyards.

I am, to be sure, a Chesapeake Bay boy from way back, and it seems my path and that of the Bay's infamous blue crab have always crossed. As a child it was when a renegade crab escaped from a bushel basket in the family kitchen and the crab and I would meet eye to eye and then run from each other in sheer terror. As a teen I spent hours checking and rechecking baited lines hanging off piers in an attempt to catch my fill of crab. Later, as a professional chef working far from home, I decided to bring the seafood of my youth to the San Francisco Bay in Berkeley, California. There at Gertie's Chesapeake Bay Café, a renowned regional restaurant that I named after my grandmother, Gertie Cleary, Californians and homesick former Chesapeake residents were treated to the tastes of crabs, crab cakes, imperial crab, and all manner of Chesapeake fare.

And now, at the urging of my publisher and friends, I am bringing more Chesapeake crab recipes and stories for seafood aficionados both near and far. So let the feast begin!

"Out of the Bay," Baltimore Sage H. L. Mencken decreed, "Baltimore ate divinely. Any poor man could go down to the banks of the river, armed with no more than a length of stout cord, a home-made net on a pole, and a chunk of cat's meat, and come home in a couple of hours with enough crabs to feed his family."

I don't know about "cat's meat," but generations of locals have been using eel, chicken necks, and the like for bait to catch enough blue crabs to pile picnic tables sky-high with steamed crustaceans for family and friends.

As each Memorial Day approaches, we Chesapeake Bay folk emerge from our winter hibernation filled with a sense of excitement that is almost unbearable. Oak trees are full with newly formed leaves; azaleas are in bloom; people perched precariously atop ladders are hanging screen windows; and warming breezes are blowing away the evening chill. All sure signs that summer is coming. And summer means no school, carefree lazy days, and, most importantly, blue crab!

Our Chesapeake Bay blue crab, or *Callinectes sapidus*, "the beautiful (savory) swimmer," is a quick, alert, feisty little scrapper. It is synonymous with the Chesapeake, an icon emblazed on signs, billboards, trucks, flags, and T-shirts all along the Bay's thousands of shoreline miles.

Although we may claim the blue crab as our own, to be perfectly honest its true range stretches from Rhode Island to Florida and the Gulf of Mexico. Statistics indicate that 50 percent of the weight of the total crab catch in the United States is blue crab; of that amount, 90 percent comes from the Chesapeake Bay. We feel reasonably sure that this means the blue crab likes the Chesapeake best! And a better neighborhood the blue couldn't ask for. The Chesapeake's many tributaries, salinity, and marsh grasses provide the perfect conditions for the blue's propagation and thriving numbers.

With the arrival of spring, the watermen have put up their dredges and tongs from the oyster season and have baited their crab pots for the opening of crabbing season on the Bay. For these rugged watermen, the blue crab is the most reliable catch of the yearly fishing season. It is the basis of a prosperous seafood industry.

Chesapeake Bay watermen, it seems, have an inherent knowledge of the blue crabs' behavior and sometimes unreliable habits. During their ten- to fifteen-hour workdays, the watermen can tell what the crabs are up to by the wind direction, the phases of the moon, and, sometimes, by just plain sniffing 'em out. They have conjured up countless names for the crustaceans over the last hundred years or so: jimmies, sooks, peelers, softs, she-crabs, buckrams, doublers. The list goes on and on.

Jimmies are male crabs. They are the best type to use for steaming and can be distinguished from the females by an inverted T shape on their underside. Sooks, the girls (immature females), have a V-shaped apron, while the she-crabs, or mature females, have a fuller, rounded apron. The females mostly end up in the picking plants, where their meat is removed from the shells to be sold as crabmeat. That's the boys and the girls of it.

There's also the matter of hard-shells and soft-shells. These are the same crab, but at different stages of growth. Blue crabs are in the "hard" stage most of the time. As they grow, they shed their shells (molt) up to twenty-three times in their three-year life-span. Each molting results in a 25 to 40 percent increase in shell size. So, to make a long story short, a soft-shell is a blue crab that has just molted and backed out of its shell.

The harvesting of soft-shell crabs is a painstaking task. The watermen can discern when a crab is about ready to molt by markings on the body and legs. These crabs, which are dubbed peelers, are moved to holding floats where they are constantly checked to see when they shed their shells. Once the shells are discarded, the crabs are taken out of the water, which stops the process of the rehardening of the shell. They are then graded according to size, packed, and shipped. What started out as a small cottage industry less than a hundred years ago is now one of the biggest seafood businesses of the Bay. (See page 17 for more information on soft-shell crabs.)

The blue crab, along with the oyster, has been one of the major culinary influences of the Chesapeake region. The crab cakes of the Baltimore and Ohio dining cars are legendary. During the twenties, deviled crab was all the rage on the eastern seaboard, keeping the Chesapeake's crab pickers working around the clock.

The locals' ethnic heritages helped shape the crab dishes of the Chesapeake. There are English- and French-style soups, bisques, and soufflés; the African-American–inspired gumbos and Creole-based dishes that have spiced up America's kitchens; and many pastas and crab-laden sauces from Italy and the Mediterranean.

The blue crab has been and always will be a key element in the cooking and eating lives of Chesapeake Bay natives. We steam 'em, fry 'em, fritter 'em . . . in the shell, out of the shell, or soft-shell. To put it mildly, if you can't already tell, we love 'em!

Browse, if you will, through these crabby recipes, and listen to some tall shellfish tales at the same time. And please, prepare and enjoy some of the extraordinary edibles from our "land of pleasant living," the home of the beautiful swimmers.

Megan Gardner
Kingsville Elementary School
Grade 5
Kingsville, Maryland

· Crabformation ·

*Soft-shell crabs and "peelers" (soft-shells in waiting) scurry about
in an emptied float where they are checked regularly
for market-readiness.*

Blue crab season on the Chesapeake runs from the beginning of May through sometime in early October, depending upon the weather. There are almost as many methods and strategies for luring the blue crabs from the Bay waters as there are crabbers. The commercial fishermen generally use trotlines, long lines, baited at intervals, that run along the bottom of the water and are anchored on both ends. Or they use crab pots, baited, mazelike traps that are quite easy for the crabs to get into, but darn near impossible for them to get out of.

Seasoned sports crabbers also usually employ these two crabbing procedures. Weekend crabbers are, however, a different story. These carefree crabbers will try almost anything to seduce the blues. They crab from bridges, off piers and docks, and from the edge of the water. Chicken neckers is their trade name and they are responsible for a large percentage of the crabs caught for backyard crab feasts.

Buck and Ty Rabuck, a veteran father-and-son crabbing team, have spent many successful years on the Bay pursuing their crabbing endeavors. This delights their neighbors in Dundalk, Maryland, for they reap the fruits of the guys' toil at huge crab feasts Buck hosts in his backyard.

Buck says the best crabbing is in the very early morning, the evenings, or in rainy weather, and that after spending long hours on the water "it gets you in the chest," producing wheezing coughs. No big problem, for the Rabucks are a crabbing family from way back, and Buck's got the "cure." So if you've been out in the elements, whether crabbing or not, and a cough sets in, or even a little congestion, try this.

Grandpap Rabuck's Rock and Rye or "Crab-Cough" Cough Syrup

2 ounces glycerine
2 ounces rock candy
1 pint rye whiskey (Pikesville brand works real good)

"The rock candy cuts the phlegm in your throat, the glycerine is a healing agent, and the rye whiskey makes it drinkable. For medicinal purposes only: Take 1 shot a day, sometimes 2 if you're feeling real poorly."

Lawrence "Buck" Rabuck, patriarch of the crabbin' Rabuck clan, has perfected a sure-fire cure for a waterman's damp weather cough—his Rock and Rye cough syrup.

· The Meat of the Matter ·

For the weak of heart or not so nimble of finger, blue crab is cooked, picked, and sold in containers for all your favorite crab recipes. The meat is graded according to the part of the crab from which it was procured.

Crabmeat is sold fresh, which is the best; pasteurized, which is the next best; and frozen, which will do nicely, although some of the flavor is lost. There are five grades:

LUMP is all big pieces from the backfin with absolutely no shell or cartilage. The best!

BACKFIN is large lump pieces along with some broken body meat.

SPECIAL OR REGULAR is the white meat from the body of the crab; it requires careful picking.

CLAW is the dark, sweet meat of the crab; it's excellent for soups, chowders, and stews.

COCKTAIL CLAW is the large claw of the crab that is sold intact, with the tip left on for dipping in sauces.

A blue crab must have a shell at least 5 inches long to be a legal catch. If it doesn't measure up, it's back to the Bay until the crustacean has moulted several more times and added more girth to its shell.

· The "Other" Crabs ·

Although many connoisseurs regard the blue crab as the best crab on the market, this is a matter of taste dictated by individual preference and geographic location. There are other excellent crab varieties harvested and available in North America.

DUNGENESS CRAB is a much larger crab than the blue. It weighs anywhere from 1 1/2 pounds to 4 pounds or more. From the Pacific Coast, it is sold live, boiled, or as picked meat.

ALASKAN KING CRAB is generally offered to consumers frozen, or previously frozen, in the form of legs and claws.

STONE CRAB is a renowned Florida crab of which only the claws are sold.

IMITATION CRAB is just that—a bit of pressed, tinted, and flavored fish.

CANNED CRAB is the tuna of the crab world. Different varieties are canned in many parts of the globe and sold in the United States.

Skateboarding, guitar-playing Ben Kraft of Parkville, Maryland, is also fast emerging on the Bay's poetry scene with his rather hip crab-beat poems.

Most of the just-mentioned varieties and products may be used as a pound-for-pound substitute for the blue crabmeat called for in the following recipes. Although I may be a stickler for using only blue crab in my kitchen, keep in mind that I'm a Chesapeake Bay boy and that's where my loyalties lie. Many of my friends whose culinary skills I greatly respect swear by the crab of their regions. As the French so aptly profess, *Vive la différence!* Do try other crab varieties if blue crab is not available in your area. The resulting dishes will be quite tasty and tremendously satisfying.

Ode to da Blue Crabie

There once was a crab who lived east.
Who had no problems and lived in peace.
Then came John the Fisherman.
Who grabbed his net and pitched him in.
Now he is part of our feast. Burp!!

Ben Kraft
Parkville Senior High School
Grade 11
Parkville, Maryland

• The Chesapeake Bay Crab Feast •

HAPPY 4th. OF JULY FROM THE RABUCK FAMILY

*The most venerable of Chesapeake culinary traditions is the
backyard crab feast, and nobody does it better than the Rabuck
clan of Dundalk, Maryland. Buck Rabuck and son Ty, center, go
out crabbing and bring home enough blue crabs to feed their
family and the better part of the neighborhood.*

O h, Lord a'mighty, it's August and so hot and humid that it's a challenge just to get from the hammock to the iced tea pitcher. As locals prop themselves up in backyard chaise lounges and watch their kids run through sprinklers, a Chesapeake spirit comes wisping through the neighborhood and takes possession of heretofore rational souls. Crabs! Hot steamed crabs! Big ole heavy jimmie crabs full of meat and encrusted with Old Bay spices! Once the spirit's got hold, you just *have* to have your fill of those succulent creatures, no ifs, ands, or buts. A person who just moments before was laid low with near heat prostration leaps from a lounge chair and starts the preparations. Phone wires burn as the crab-alert is sounded to friends and family from town to town. There's gonna be a crustacean revival and plans must be made. Whether it be the home crab pot fired up or everyone meeting at a Chesapeake crab house, come hell or high water there'll be a crab feast tonight!

There once was a crab named Jab which was a real cad. That was real mad. He wanted some food that was good so he Jabbed another crab that tastrd bad then he was even morr mad. Then he swam to his pad then he got hookrd he jabbed the lad that lowered the line then he jumped on his dad who got a tad mad at the lad who got jabbed which had much mad for the crab—Jab.

Jonas Cadwallader
Kingsville Elementary School
Grade 5
Kingsville, Maryland

On Route 40 of Maryland's Eastern Shore, a review of dancing crabs greets guests ready to feast at the Old Mill Crab House.

The crab feast of the Chesapeake Bay is a traditional gathering, much in the same way as clambakes are in New England or barbecues are in Texas. Folks get together to feast on and celebrate the most prized gift of the Chesapeake, the blue crab. During the summer months there's always a party going on, with steamed crabs piled high, beer flowing freely, and the smell of spicy crab seasonings wafting through the humid summer air. These crab-picking assemblies congregate in

How to Eat Crabs

First you take off the claws. Then you Break the claws in two pieces. Secondly, you Break the shell off of the crab. Then you remove the lungs, but don't eat them. Eat the meat instead.

Erik Bowles
Kingsville Elementary School
Grade 5
Kingsville, Maryland

Mike Eberhardt
Parkville Senior High School
Grade 11
Parkville, Maryland

Kenny Opdyke
Kingsville Elementary School
Grade 5
Kingsville, Maryland

parks, at festivals, in backyards, at the shore, on farms, at apartment complexes, or at one of the world-famous crab houses of the Chesapeake.

At a Gunning's Crab House Veteran Waitresses (Sharon Willis, Vickie Leonard, and Rene Kline) Symposium and Confab on the ins-and-outs of picking, slinging, and other blue crab matters, waitress Vickie, after discussing countless crab-picking techniques, leaned over to me and asked in dead earnest, "Can you even remember anybody teaching you *how* to eat crabs? You just figure you're born knowing *how!*" No, Vickie, I don't remember. And I believe that if you put that question to just about any Chesapeake native, you'd get the same answer. We accept it as a skill genetically bestowed upon Chesapeakeans.

I suppose that most natives' crab skills were honed at neighborhood crab feasts, where generations of crab pickers screamed, sang, picked, and imparted their crab wisdom to the younger generation. You learned how to pick up the live crabs destined for the steaming pots, hopefully without getting bitten.

Then there were anatomy lessons from great-aunts and uncles. "Now this here's the 'devil.' Look at it. It'll kill you! Don't you ever eat it, you hear me?" Of course I wouldn't eat it! Hell, I didn't even want to touch it.

Or late in the evening, when the backyard feasts were over, kids would be busy chasing lightning bugs and the bells of the ice cream man could be heard in the distance. That's when Aunt Treasie would perk up and grab the nearest child by the elastic waistband of his Bermuda shorts, pull him over to her lawn chair, and declare, "Do you know that if you eat ice cream right after you eat crabs, you'll get sick as a dog? Yeah! 'Em crabs 'll turn to rock, right in your stomach! Yes siree, sick as a dog!" All the other elders would nod their heads in silent agreement. Now where did they come up with that one? But it stuck. To this day, I don't know even one of my young crab-picking compatriots who actually ever dared to put the ice cream theory to the test.

New to the crazy let-your-hair-down, all-hell-has-broken-loose world of crab feasts? Don't worry. Take yourself on down to one of the many Chesapeake's crab

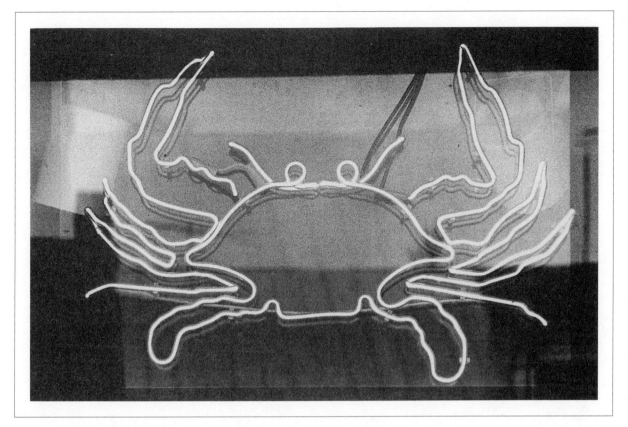

A neon crustacean beckons customers
to a Chesapeake seafood market.

houses, where "the girls," those seasoned experts of the crab hackeries, will be your personalized tutors in the art of crab picking.

Now if you're a businessman, you will be instructed to first remove your coat and tie. Next, roll up those sleeves or you'll look like a rookie. Okay, now you're dressed properly. Take a deep breath and let it out slowly. Let go of your inhibitions. The idea here is to make a big mess. "Go to town, hon. The dirtier you get, the better you'll like them crabs!"

(Note on *hon*. All the waitresses in the crab houses call everybody hon. It's a tradition. Next thing that happens is that you start calling the waitress hon in response, and then very soon everyone at the table is calling each other hon. It's a very catchy endearment.)

Crabs are steamed with spicy seasonings that coat the shell. Do not ask for these spices to be washed off. Your ignorance will show. " 'At's the good stuff on 'air, hon. It tastes great."

Sleeves up? Let's go!

Here is an official set of crab-picking instructions from a Chesapeake Bay crab house. Remember, though, you'll find as many methods for crab picking as you find waitresses. They all have their favorite techniques.

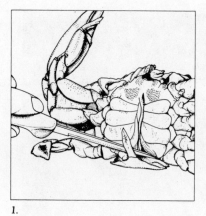

1.

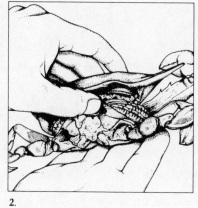

2.

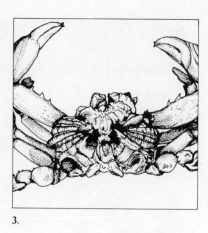

3.

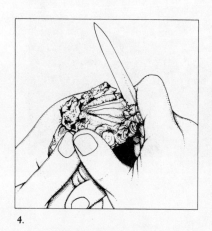

4.

5.

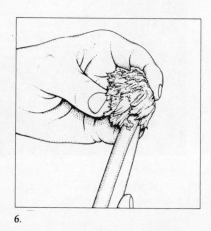

6.

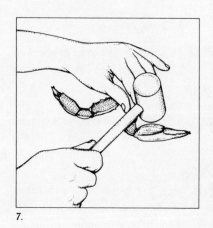

7.

1. *With knife tip or finger remove apron.*

2. *Remove top shell with thumb or tip of crab knife or paring knife.*

3. *Pull off claws and set aside for eating later. Remove swimming legs and back fins. Cut away eyes and remove gills. Scrape out greenish matter (the devil), running through center of crab, but leave yellow "mustard."*

4. *With crab knife or paring knife, cut away edges around circumference of crab's body. Holding crab in two hands, break in half down the center.*

5. *Cut each half again horizontally to expose the chamber of crabmeat.*

6. *With tip of crab knife or paring knife, pick out lumps of crabmeat and enjoy.*

7. *With a mallet or handle of heavy table knife, crack claws and pick out meat. (Some folks like to use a crab knife during this process. Knife is placed across claw and driven into shell by mallet to crack it.)*

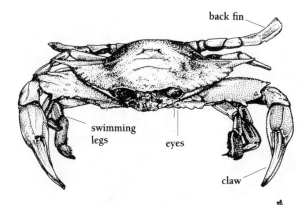

back fin

swimming
legs

eyes

claw

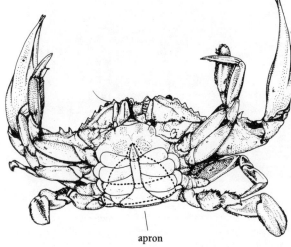

apron

The shape of the apron on the underside of the crab, which is the first part of the crab shell that is removed in the picking process, distinguishes a male from a female. We have shown the shape of a female crab's apron with a dotted line superimposed over a male's apron.

• Have the crabs unceremoniously dumped on the newspaper or brown paper.
• Flip the crab over.
• Flip open the apron.
• Flip off the top shell. ("It's like a flip top!")
• You will now notice "all this stuff hanging out, the devil and a bunch of guts."
• Pull the devil and guts out; throw them on the newspaper. Remember, that's what the paper's for.
• The yellow stuff in the middle is the "mustard." Actually it's fat and quite delicious. Eat it.
• Break the body in half, leaving the legs and claws on.
• "Squish down the backfin end, and twist it around. You'll get a big piece of backfin meat." Um good!
• Pull the swimming legs and claws off of the body, one by one. There will be a little piece of meat at the end of each. Suck it. Save the claws.
• Take the paring knife and split each half of the crab through horizontally. This exposes chambers of crab-meat. Use the paring knife to pick out the meat.
• Now here comes the mallet! Take a big claw and break it apart at the joint. Break each half in two by using the mallet to drive the paring knife through the claw, and gently pull out a whole piece of claw meat. This takes practice.

Keep repeating the above steps until you've eaten your fill. Remember that practice makes perfect, and before you know it you'll be picking crabs like one of the gals down to the picking plants. Happy picking, hon!

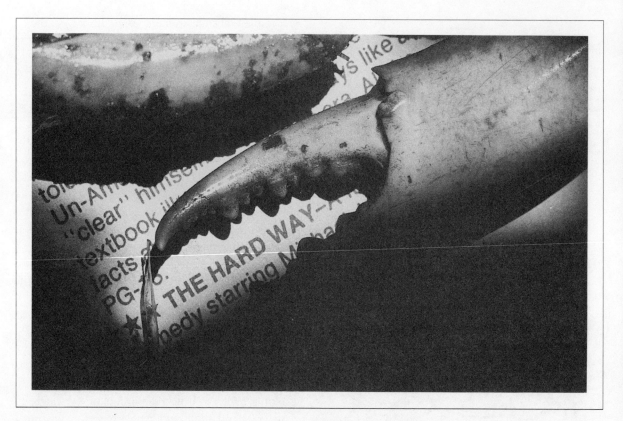

Glossary of Feast Equipment and Lingo

Brown paper or newspapers are the tablecloths of choice when sitting down to steamed crabs. Locals like this method because it makes for an easy cleanup. Sprinkle the leftover shells with a little laundry detergent before rolling up the papers, so the shells don't stink up your trash can.

NEWSPAPERS are the ritualistic covering for the feast table. They are practical because during the meal you throw everything right onto the paper, and when the feast is complete, you just roll the whole shebang up. A little hint in case the trashman's not coming around for a day or two: Sprinkle some soap powder (Tide's good) over the top of all the crab shells before rolling the paper up. It keeps the stink down.

MALLETS are *not* for smashing up the crabs into little bits with the hope of getting to the meat. All you would accomplish with this is looking like a rank novice, and crabmeat full of shell fragments. The mallets are for gently cracking the crabs' claws so that full pieces of meat will emerge.

PARING KNIVES are quite handy for cutting the crab body in half to expose the chambers of meat, and for picking the meat out with the tip of the knife.

COLD BEER is the crab pickers' all-time favorite beverage. I can't smell one without thinking of the other.

ICE COLD GINGER ALE is the drink for beer abstainers, kids, and designated drivers.

LUNGS are the gills, or spongy mass, exposed when the top shell is removed.

GUTS is a not-so-glamorous, self-explanatory, but graphically accurate description of a crab's intestinal area. See also devil.

DEVIL is another term for the innards and guts. This is also the entity you may meet face-to-face if you insist on eating this part of the crab.

DEAD MAN is a one-step-beyond synonym of guts and devil, denoting the legendary end result.

MUSTARD is the yellowish matter in the center of the crab body. It is the crab's fat. This is some good eating!

SWIMMING LEGS are the small legs of the crab.

FLIPPERS are the rear propellers of the crab.

So on with the show! Here are two versions for you do-it-yourself crab feasters.

Steamed Blue Crabs

Serves 2 to 3 novice pickers, 2 intermediates, or 1 hungry pro

This is the traditional Chesapeake Bay method for the steamed blue crab feast.

Two 12-ounce cans beer, allowed to go flat
2 cups distilled white vinegar
12 live large male blue crabs (jimmies)
1/2 cup Old Bay seasoning
6 tablespoons salt (kosher style is best)

In a steamer pot or large, heavy pot with a tight-fitting lid, mix together the beer and vinegar. Put a round raised rack into the pot that is tall enough to clear the liquid. Bring to a good strong boil.

While the pot is coming to a boil, you may, if desired, fill a tub with ice water and put the crabs into it for 5 minutes or so. This icing process is used by crab houses and veteran crab steamers. The cold bath numbs the crabs, making them easier to handle. It also keeps the crabs from losing their claws during the steaming process. The third advantage is that the seasonings stick to the shells better.

Mix the Old Bay and salt together in a small bowl. Place a layer of crabs on the rack in the pot. Sprinkle with a generous coating of the seasoning. Continue layering and seasoning the crabs until all the blues are in the pot and you have used up all the seasoning. Put on the lid and steam over moderately high heat until the crabs are bright red, about 25 minutes.

Serve hot. Leftover crabs may be refrigerated and either eaten cold the next day or picked for crabmeat to use in your favorite recipe.

"How To Crack a Crab"

Step 1: Buy barbecue potatoe chips.
Step 2: Prepare sauce . . . Soy sauce with melted Parkay butter.
Step 3: Buy a box of Ritz crackers.
Step 4: Eat the legs of the crab (rear first).
Step 5: Dip meat into mixture of soy sauce and melted butter.
Step 6: Eat the center (the meat).
Step 7: Ritz time! Take another crab and put the meat in the mixture and eat the solution on two Ritz crackers.
Step 8: Squeeze juice from legs of crabs and put on potato chips.
Step 9: Eat it all up! (Suck "dead man").
Hint: Between steps 4–9 drink water!

Patrese Taylor
Parkville Senior High School
Grade 11
Parkville, Maryland

Montbray Supreme Steamed Hard-Shell Blue Crabs

Makes "enough to take 4 people to Gourmet Heaven"

Gourmet steamed crabs on the Chesapeake? You bet! Here's how they are prepared by G. Hamilton Mowbray, a columnist for the American Wine Society Journal *and the founder of Montbray Vineyards. The vineyard, the oldest continuously operated family winery in Maryland, is situated in Carroll County's Silver Run Valley. Mr. Mowbray suggests a bottle or two of Maryland Seyve-Villard, a dry white table wine, with these elegant crustaceans.*

1 bottle (1 fifth/750 ml) dry white wine
1 cup water
24 live large male blue crabs (jimmies)
1/4 cup salt
2 tablespoons ground black pepper

In a steamer pot or large, heavy pot with a tight-fitting lid, mix the wine and water. Place a round raised rack into the pot that is tall enough to clear the liquid. Bring to a good strong boil.

Place a layer of crabs on the rack in the pot. Sprinkle with some of the salt and pepper. Continue layering and seasoning until all the blues are in the pot and you have used up all the seasoning. Put on the lid and steam over moderately high heat until the crabs are bright red, about 25 minutes.

Serve hot.

Opposite: On the side of the road along Glen Burnie, Maryland's Ritchie Highway, a peering crab eyes passing motorists. Once this crabby fellow was adorned with hundreds of small lights, but due to state law he can no longer be lit for fear of accidents caused by rubbernecking drivers paying more attention to the crab than the road.

Notes on Crab Feast Accompaniments

At a crab feast, many people enjoy eating crabs and nothing else. Each clan has its own traditions, however. Here are some ideas.

• Serve bowls of vinegar (apple or red wine) for dipping the picked crabmeat.
• Serve melted butter for dipping. Lobster fans and out-of-towners are quite fond of this pairing. It's not the traditional Chesapeake way, but it is tasty.
• Platters of sliced tomatoes.
• Mounds of sweet corn on the cob.
• Assorted salads such as coleslaw, potato, macaroni, or marinated vegetables.
• Desserts are not traditionally served but could include strawberry shortcake, lemon meringue pie, peach cake, watermelon, or pickled watermelon rind. Remember, no ice cream! According to Chesapeake lore this could be hazardous to your health (page 8).

· Soft-Shell Crabs ·

A car's headlights illuminate a soft-shell crab sign on Smith Island at Knapp's Narrows.

In the brackish waters of the Chesapeake's marsh grasses, from the first full moon of May throughout the summer and into the fall, the blue crabs go through their remarkable growth process of molting.

It is at this stage, when the crabs have just backed out of their shells, that the soft-shell emerges. During a blue crab's average three-year life-span, it may shed its shell up to twenty-three times. These moltings are the basis of the soft-shell crab industry, which is centered in Crisfield, Maryland.

The Chesapeake Bay accounts for 90 percent of the United States soft-shell crab production. This traditional crustacean of the South, the Chesapeake's most precious culinary emissary, is shipped around the globe to all the great gastronomic centers.

Soft-shell crabs are sold fresh (live) and frozen. The far superior product is, of course, the former. Frozen soft-shells are fine for deep-frying or for adding to a soup or chowder, but they do not retain the delicate flavor of the fresh.

Soft-shells are referred to by a number of terms, including softs, peelers, red signs, ranks, busters, buckrams, paper shells, Sally crabs, and snots. Most of these names come from the Chesapeake's watermen, who use the monikers to denote the various stages of the soft's molting.

Thought of as opulent dining in the rest of the world, soft-shells are just as "common as crabs" to the locals.

During the summer months, fried softs can be found on virtually every menu, from fancy dinnerhouse to plain-jane coffee shop. Neighborhood kids sit on front stoops munching soft-shell sandwiches, with little crab legs dangling out of the edges of white bread. If it's summer, it's soft-shell time, and that's eating just about as good as it gets.

Soft-shells are graded by the size of the shell span:

Mediums	3 1/2 to 4 inches
Hotels	4 to 4 1/2 inches
Primes	4 1/2 to 5 inches
Jumbos	5 to 5 1/2 inches
Whales	5 1/2 inches and up

Dressing a Soft-shell Crab

- Use soft-shell crabs that are alive and "kicking."
- Wash the crabs with cold water.
- Cut off eyes with scissors. (Cut straight across the face, about 1/4 inch behind the eyes.)
- Remove the apron from the underside of the crab.
- Lift the pointed ends of the shell upward and out, and pull or snip out the spongy gills.
- Dry the crabs and prepare as desired.

Handy's Beer-Battered Softs

Serves 4

For over seventy-five years, the John T. Handy Company has been the world's largest producer of soft-shell crabs. Nelda DiLauro provided this tempura batter–like family recipe, a favorite of the Handy company.

1 1/4 cups all-purpose flour, plus about 1/2 cup for dusting softs
2 teaspoons salt
1/2 teaspoon baking powder
1 teaspoon paprika

One 12-ounce bottle beer, allowed to go flat, at room temperature
8 prime or jumbo soft-shell crabs, cleaned (page 17)
Vegetable oil for deep-frying

In a mixing bowl sift together the flour, salt, and baking powder. Mix in the paprika. Slowly mix in the beer to make a smooth batter. Let the batter stand at room temperature for 1 to 2 hours since it thickens as it stands.

Lightly dust the softs with the flour, gently shaking off any excess. Pour oil into a deep skillet or deep-fat fryer and heat to 375°F. Dip each crab in the batter to coat evenly and then slip it into the hot oil; do not crowd the pan. Deep-fry until golden brown, 3 to 5 minutes. Remove to paper towels to drain briefly. Serve at once.

Harrison "Jabo" Lake, 74, an employee of the John T. Handy Company in Crisfield, Maryland, runs his fingers over dozens of packaged soft-shell crabs and in seconds can tell if one isn't quite right. According to co-workers, "It isn't a Handy crab 'til Jabo says it's a Handy crab!"

Soft Crab Moutarde

Serves 4

These mustard-enchanced soft-shells are a slightly pungent taste treat, with the crisp exterior of a panfried crab, topped by a garlicky lemon butter sauce.

8 prime soft-shell crabs, cleaned (page 17)
1/4 cup Dijon-style mustard
All-purpose flour seasoned with salt and ground black pepper
3 eggs, beaten
Fine dried bread crumbs

Clarified butter or olive oil for sautéing
Juice of 1 lemon
1/2 teaspoon minced garlic
1/4 pound butter
2 tablespoons chopped fresh parsley

Coat both sides of the softs with the mustard and refrigerate for 1 hour.

Lightly dust the crabs with the seasoned flour, shaking off any excess. Dip them in the eggs and then roll them in the bread crumbs.

Heat the clarified butter or oil in a sauté pan until golden brown, over medium-heat. Add the softs and cook about 3 minutes on each side. Remove to paper towels to drain and keep warm.

Discard the fat from the pan and return the pan to medium heat. Add the lemon juice and deglaze the pan, scraping up all the browned bits. Add the garlic and reduce the heat to low. Whisk in the butter, bit by bit. Stir in the parsley. Spoon the sauce over the crabs and serve hot.

Soft-Shell Crab Sandwich

Serves 4

"Oh, my Gawd! There're little legs dangling out the sides of that sandwich." You won't find soft-shell crab sandwiches assembled in many places outside of Chesapeake country, but softs actually make for a unique sandwich sensation. They both please your palate and tickle your lips. And that's a claim very few sandwiches can make.

4 jumbo or whale soft-shell crabs, cleaned (page 17)
8 slices good-quality white bread
Mayonnaise or Tartar Sauce (page 20)

4 large slices ripe tomato
Salt and ground black pepper
4 leaves lettuce

First, fry the soft-shells. The method used in "No Bullhocky" Fried Soft-Shells (page 20) will do nicely. Then drain them on paper towels.

Lather the bread slices with mayonnaise or Tartar Sauce. Place a crab on each of 4 slices of the bread. Top each crab with a tomato slice, sprinkle with salt and pepper to taste, and then crown with a lettuce leaf. Put on the top bread slices and enjoy!

"No Bullhocky" Fried Soft-Shells

Serves 4

My friend Ollie Reese, a Susque-hanna River boy, doesn't take too kindly to fancy soft-shell prepa-rations. Just thinking about sau-téed crabs with this and that on them sends his nerves all to hell. Here's his no-muss, no-fuss rec-ipe. He figures that if you fry them up like this, you'll never eat them any other way.

8 prime soft-shell crabs, cleaned (page 17)
All-purpose flour seasoned with salt, ground black pepper, and a touch of cayenne pepper

Solid vegetable shortening for frying
Tartar Sauce (recipe follows)
Lemon wedges (optional)

Give the softs a good dose of seasoned flour.

In a cast-iron or other heavy skillet, melt enough shortening so that it is about 1 inch deep, then get it good and hot. Fry the crabs until golden brown, 3 to 4 minutes on each side. Remove with tongs or a slotted spoon to paper towels to drain and then go to town.

Serve with Tartar Sauce and lemon wedges if you're so inclined.

Tartar Sauce

Makes 1 1/2 cups

1 cup mayonnaise
1/2 cup finely chopped dill pickle
1/4 cup minced onion

2 tablespoons chopped fresh parsley
1 tablespoon dill pickle juice

Mix all ingredients together in a bowl. Chill for at least one hour before serving.

Shirley's Bait Shack on Deal Island off Maryland's Eastern Shore has its own kind of down-home charm with a decorating scheme of crab pots, bushel baskets, and buoys.

Christine Marshall of Marion, Maryland, works for Frank's Seafood in Crisfield tending the soft-shell floats during the season. She averages one-and-one-half hours of sleep a night during the peak season. The rest of her time is devoted to searching the 120 floats, each of which contains 400 to 800 crabs, for peelers and soft-shell crabs.

Soft-Shells Stuffed with Imperial

Serves 4

Chesapeake seafood restaurants often feature this extravagant dish as a summertime special. The experience of biting into the slightly crunchy soft-shells, followed by a burst of the rich imperial stuffing titillating your taste buds, is, as the old saying goes, "like heaven and earth coming together!"

1/2 batch of your favorite imperial recipe (pages 69 to 71)
Hollandaise Sauce (optional; page 36)

8 prime or jumbo soft-shell crabs, cleaned (page 17)
Clarified butter
Lemon wedges

Prepare the imperial and put aside. Prepare the sauce and keep warm. Preheat the broiler.

Stuff some of the imperial mixture under the sides and center of the top shell of each soft. Lightly grease a broiler pan with the butter and place the crabs on the pan, top shell up. Brush the crabs liberally with the butter. Slip the pan into the broiler, about 4 inches from the flame, and broil, carefully turning several times to brown both sides, until done, 6 to 8 minutes.

Top with hollandaise and lemon wedges and serve at once.

Busters Béarnaise

Serves 4

Buster is a term used to denote an extremely small soft-shell crab. This recipe has New Orleans origins and folks down that way actually use busters and consider them a soft-shell delicacy. Around the Chesapeake you'll be hard pressed to find buster-sized softs because of size limits imposed by the watermen. So busters or not, any smaller-sized soft-shell will do nicely for this delicious preparation.

Béarnaise Sauce (recipe follows)
12 very small soft-shell crabs, cleaned (page 17)
All-purpose flour seasoned with salt, ground black pepper, and a touch of cayenne pepper

4 tablespoons butter
2 tablespoons olive oil
Juice of 1 lemon
2 tablespoons chopped fresh parsley

Prepare the sauce and keep warm.

Lightly dust the softs with the seasoned flour, shaking off any excess.

In a large skillet over medium-high heat, warm the butter and oil. Add the soft-shells and sauté for about 3 minutes on each side. Remove the crabs to a heated platter. Pour off half of the cooking fat.

Return the pan to the heat and add the lemon juice and parsley. Heat for 1 minute and then pour over the crabs.

Top each serving with some of the Béarnaise Sauce.

Béarnaise Sauce

Makes about 1 1/4 cups

1/2 cup white wine vinegar
4 shallots, minced
2 tablespoons minced fresh tarragon
3 whole black peppercorns
Pinch of salt

4 egg yolks
1 tablespoon boiling water
1 cut clarified butter, heated
Juice of 1/2 lemon
Chopped fresh tarragon or parsley (optional)

In a small saucepan combine the vinegar, shallots, tarragon, peppercorns, and salt. Bring to a boil and cook until almost all of the liquid has evaporated. Set aside and allow to cool to room temperature.

Place the egg yolks in a stainless-steel mixing bowl. Add the tarragon reduction and the boiling water. Whisk together well. Place the mixing bowl over top a pot of simmering water. Whisk constantly, until the mixture becomes pale and creamy. Remove from the heat and gradually whisk in the clarified butter to make a thick sauce. (When combining the butter and the egg mixture, they should be the same temperature.) Beat in the lemon juice and strain sauce through a fine sieve.

A little chopped fresh tarragon or parsley may be added if you like. Keep warm.

Blackened Soft-Shells

Serves 4

Soft-shells lend themselves well to blackening because they need to cook only a short time. The flavorful herb butter embellishes the aromatic blackening spices as well as adding moisture to the finished crabs. This dish goes well with a Cajun- or pilaf-style rice.

Herb Mustard Butter (recipe follows)
8 prime soft-shell crabs, cleaned (page 17)
1 cup clarified butter, melted and cooled

Cajun Blackening Spice (page 39) or Old Bay seasoning for blackening (about 1/2 cup)

Prepare the Herb Mustard Butter and refrigerate until firm.

Heat a large cast-iron skillet over high heat until smoking hot (the hotter the better).

Dip the crabs in the clarified butter and then lightly coat them with the seasoning. Place each crab, top shell down, in the skillet. Cook for 2 to 3 minutes, then turn and cook on the second side for 2 to 3 minutes.

Place the crabs on warmed plates. Top each with a pat of Herb Mustard Butter. Serve at once.

NOTE: Whenever using this blackening method, be sure you are working in a well-ventilated area. This process produces a lot of smoke, so put on the exhaust fan and open the windows or the smoke alarms will be wailing.

Herb Mustard Butter

Makes about 1 cup

This makes more butter than is needed for the softs, but it is great to have on hand to top grilled fish fillets or grilled meats such as steaks, chops, or chicken breasts.

1/2 pound salted butter, softened
3 tablespoons Dijon-style mustard
1/4 teaspoon minced garlic
1/4 teaspoon minced shallot
3 leaves fresh sage, finely chopped

2 large leaves fresh basil, finely chopped
3 sprigs fresh chives, minced
3 tablespoons chopped fresh parsley
Juice of 1 lemon
Freshly ground black pepper

In a mixing bowl combine all the ingredients and whip together, either by hand or by electric mixer, until well mixed. Spread the seasoned butter down the center of a length of waxed paper. Roll the butter to form a log with a width the size of a quarter. Wrap in waxed paper and refrigerate to firm up butter before cutting.

Johnny's Sautéed Softs

Serves 4

Yeah, that's me! This is my California, slightly frou-frou, soft-shell preparation created for some persnickety customers who were put off by the standard Chesapeake fried or panfried preparations. Just as well those westerners balked at "fried," because they provided the impetus for the development of this succulent recipe that makes for an impressive meal, perfect for that special occasion. Tender springtime asparagus are the perfect vegetable accompaniment for these softs.

8 prime or jumbo soft-shell crabs, cleaned (page 17)

All-purpose flour seasoned with salt and ground black pepper

8 tablespoons (1/4 pound) butter

1/4 cup olive oil

1/4 cup dry vermouth

1/4 cup Fish Stock (optional; page 61)

1 teaspoon minced garlic

Juice of 1 lemon

2 tablespoons chopped, drained capers

2 tablespoons chopped fresh basil

Salt and ground black pepper to taste

Dust the soft-shells in the seasoned flour.

In a large skillet over medium heat, melt 2 tablespoons of the butter with the oil. Add the crabs and cook, turning once, until golden, about 3 minutes on each side. Place the crabs on a platter and keep warm.

Discard the cooking oil. Return the pan to high heat, add the vermouth, and deglaze the pan, scraping up all the browned bits. Add the stock, garlic, and lemon juice. Cook until about 1/4 cup liquid remains. Reduce the heat to low and add the capers and basil. Whisk in the remaining 6 tablespoons of butter, bit by bit. Season with salt and pepper.

Spoon the sauce over the crabs and serve at once.

Sea gulls looking for handouts line the remains of an old shanty pier on Smith Island, Maryland.

Pecan-Coated Soft-Shells with Whiskey-Lemon Butter

Serves 4

A traditional crab batter is laden with toasted pecans for an exciting soft-shell variation that is enhanced with a "hootch"-infused lemon-butter sauce. Our dear Miss Alma, who was, "Gawd rest her soul," the originator of this concoction, would always confide to her dinner guests that "I really don't like using the whiskey, but my Mama told me it disinfects the crabs." So here it is, a medicinally pure and exceptionally tasty dish.

1 1/2 cups all-purpose flour, plus extra for dusting crabs
1/2 teaspoon baking powder
2 teaspoons salt
1/2 teaspoon ground black pepper
3/4 cup ice water
1/2 cup coarsely chopped toasted pecans

Vegetable oil for frying
8 soft-shell crabs, cleaned (page 17)
1/2 cup bourbon whiskey
Juice of 1 lemon
1/4 pound lightly salted butter, broken into bits
2 tablespoons chopped fresh parsley

In a bowl combine the 1 1/2 cups flour, baking powder, salt, and pepper. Slowly mix in the water to form a smooth batter. Let stand for 1 hour. When ready to use, fold in the pecans.

In a skillet, pour in oil to reach a depth of about 1/4 inch. Heat to about 375°F. Dust the softs in flour and dip in batter. Slip the crabs into the pan and fry until golden, about 3 minutes on each side. Remove to paper towels to drain and keep warm.

Discard the cooking oil. Return the pan to high heat, add the whiskey, and deglaze the pan, scraping up all the browned bits. Pour in the lemon juice and reduce the heat to low. Whisk in the butter, bit by bit. Remove from the heat and stir in the parsley.

Arrange the soft-shells on a platter. Spoon the sauce over the softs.

Watermen's Deep-Fried Buckrams

Serves 4

Buckrams are soft-shells that almost aren't; that is, their shells are nearing the hardened stage. These crabs are not readily available at markets but are found mostly in towns or locales where softs are harvested. They are a favorite of Chesapeake watermen.

1 1/2 cups all-purpose flour
2 teaspoons salt
1/2 teaspoon ground black pepper
2 eggs
1 1/2 cups milk

1 tablespoon Worcestershire sauce
3 tablespoons chopped fresh parsley
8 buckrams, cleaned (page 17)
Vegetable oil for frying

In a mixing bowl combine the flour, salt, and pepper. Stir in the eggs, milk, Worcestershire sauce, and parsley to make a fairly smooth batter.

In a skillet pour in oil until it reaches a depth of about 1/2 inch. Dip the buckrams in the batter and slip them into the pan. Fry, turning once, until golden, about 4 minutes on each side. Drain briefly on paper towels. Serve hot.

· Crab Cakes ·

At Nick's Inner Harbor Seafood stall in Baltimore's Cross Street Market, Joan Sands mixes up a batch of delicious all-lump crab cakes. Locals mob the counter, eating up the lightly fried cakes almost as fast as Joan makes them.

O h, the crab cake! A little mound of heaven right here on earth. Paris has its *foie gras,* New Orleans is gumbo heaven, and Spain is the land of *paella,* and that's just fine with the folks living along the shores and far-reaching tributaries of the Chesapeake Bay. After all, they have their own signature dish. Welcome to Crab Cake Country. No dish is more closely associated with the Chesapeake and the blue crab than the mighty crab cake.

When asked to describe their aquatic culinary prize, locals are hard pressed to come up with a concise description. "Well hon, 'tain't a confection, and you don't normally bake 'em, and sure 'tain't a dee-sert . . . naa . . . it's not exactly made in a cake pan either . . . well . . . oh hell, it's more like a ball o'crab all spiced up and fried."

Now the crab cake may well be a unifying source of fierce regional pride, almost an obsession if you will. But its many recipes produce more squabbling, feuding, and heated family debates than either the local ball club or politics.

Tucked away with each family's genealogical archives is The Crab Cake Recipe. It is the only one, it is the best, and all the others are wrong, period. I've witnessed barroom brawls over which restaurant or tavern serves the best crab cake. Research on the ubiquitous cake provides tremendous pleasure for the stomach, but is, all and all, a dangerous business.

Now, what's all the fuss about? They're just little balls of crab all mushed together, right? Wrong! Here's a guide to the structural makeup of the highly controversial crab cake.

· The Care and Handling of Crab Cakes
or How to Be Your Crab Cake's Best Friend ·

Choice of Crabmeat

This is like choosing a pedigree pet. Should it be a fancy purebred or a mixed breed? This all depends on your tastes and, in some cases, your wallet. (See page 4 for an explanation of crabmeat grades.)

LUMP CRABMEAT is what purists generally insist on for creating the perfect cake. These cakes consist of nothing but full moist lumps that deliver crab cake Nirvana. Crab cakes made with all lump are best sautéed or broiled rather than deep-fried.

BACKFIN CRABMEAT makes a beautiful cake of large, delectable lumps of crab and a bit of body meat. Just a touch of binding holds the backfin cake together nicely. These cakes are fine cooked in any style.

CLAW MEAT provides a dark, sweet, and less expensive crab cake. These cakes, while not regarded as top of the line, are what are served in many coffee shops and neighborhood taverns, as well as at local fairs and carnivals. They are quite tasty and more economical for large gatherings when many cakes will be devoured.

MIXED CAKES are constructed from a blend of two or more types of crabmeat. My favorite mix is half lump and half special, but actually any combination will work.

Try your own formulas to find what you like best.

The crab cake dishes in this book list the crabmeat grade the recipes' originators believe works best, but feel free to substitute any type of crabmeat.

Binding

These are the vehicles employed to hold together and season the crab cakes. The wet ingredients are mixed with various seasonings, tossed with the crabmeat, and held together with breading. The principle is to try to use the least amount of breading possible to get the cakes to hold together without exerting pressure to compact them. Some traditional binding ingredients are eggs, mayonnaise, cream, cream sauces, seasonings, bread crumbs, cracker crumbs, and bread soaked in milk.

Seasonings

The local seasoning concoctions—quantities of, ratios to, secret mixing methods—are the things witches' brews are made of. They can enhance or mask the crab, and may or may not bring tears to the eyes and nose. The following seasonings are also found in most other typical Chesapeake blue crab dishes.

OLD BAY SEASONING is synonymous with Chesapeake cooking and especially crabs. A staple in every Chesapeake kitchen, it is as much a required shelf item as are salt and pepper. When I opened my restaurant, Gertie's Chesapeake Bay Café, in Berkeley, California, I was swamped with calls from former Chesapeake residents wanting to know if I used Old Bay and where they could get some of this hometown memory. Old Bay is now distributed nationally by McCormick and Company (see page 92 for more information). The recipe is top secret but includes salt, pepper, mustard, pimiento, cloves, bay leaves, mace, cardamom, ginger, cassia, and paprika. Its aroma and distinctive taste set the locals' mouths a-watering and minds racing with memories of glorious Chesapeake meals.

WORCESTERSHIRE SAUCE is of English origin and is made from vinegar, molasses, garlic, anchovies, and other spices.

TABASCO SAUCE or any hot chile sauce.

LEMON JUICE

MUSTARD, including dry and prepared (Dijon-style is especially popular).

PREPARED HORSERADISH

PARSLEY

Preparation and Forming

These are the most important steps in making successful crab cakes.

PICKING Pick the crabmeat over carefully for shells. Not only carefully, but gently. The lumps of crab are the beauty of the crab cake and must not be torn apart while picking.

BATTER Make the batter (that is, the eggs, mayonnaise, seasonings) in a separate bowl, not in the same one that holds the crabmeat. Sprinkle the breading (that is, the bread crumbs or cracker crumbs) over the crabmeat and then pour the batter on top of the breading. Now, gently toss or fold the ingredients together, again taking great care not to break up the lumps of crab.

FORMING Form the crab cake mixture into slightly flattened, rounded masses. Some folks recommend gently packing the mixture into an ice cream scoop and then tapping it out. It can, of course, be formed by hand or molded into small, rounded cups. Again, *gently* is the key word when describing how to form a cake. Do not compact the crab cakes too much. They should be held together loosely. The size of the cake depends on the maker. Most cakes weigh out at about 2 1/2 to 3 ounces each. Many crab cake veterans feel it is best to refrigerate the cakes at least an hour before cooking. This allows the binding to absorb some of the moisture so that the cakes hold together better.

Cooking

FRYING is the most common cooking method for crab cakes. They can be panfried in cooking oil (usually vegetable or peanut) about 1/2 inch deep, or deep-fried, with the oil heated to 375°F.

SAUTÉING is high-class crab cake cooking, generally using clarified butter, olive oil, or a combination of the two.

BROILING is one of the best ways to cook cakes, because the flavor of the crab does not have to compete with that of the cooking oil. All you need to do is brush the cakes with a little melted butter if desired and place them about 3 inches from the flame in a preheated broiler. Plan on broiling about 5 to 6 minutes.

Sauces

Locals are also quite opinionated about what type of sauce, if any, should be served with crab cakes. Lemon wedges are always served with cakes and actually provide the simplest and most taste-enhancing topping to be found. A few preferred sauces follow.

TARTAR SAUCE (page 20) is the most traditional crab cake enhancer. As ketchup is to french fries, so tartar sauce is to crab cakes.

MUSTARD, either a prepared, horseradish-laden type, or nowadays even that fancy French Dijon-style.

RED WINE VINEGAR OR CIDER VINEGAR, just a dab will do ya.

REMOULADE (page 35) is a Cajun-style tartar sauce that is a nice change with cakes.

HOLLANDAISE SAUCE (page 36) and other sauces from the hollandaise family are impressive with a fancy crab cake dinner.

Accompaniments

At restaurants and taverns along the Bay, most crab cakes are served with crispy French fries and mounds of fresh coleslaw. However, at home everyone has their own favorite accompaniment. Here are a few of the most popular.

SALTINES . . . that's right, hon! And don't forget them. Sit a piece of cake atop the cracker and go for it!
FRENCH FRIES
COLESLAW
POTATO SALAD
SLICED RIPE TOMATOES
FRESH ASPARAGUS
CUCUMBER SALAD
CORN ON THE COB
CORN BREAD
BISCUITS
   And on and on. Start your own traditions!

Gertie's Crab Cakes

Serves 4

Gertie Cleary hailed from Baltimore's Greenmount Avenue, and her cooking was legendary throughout St. Ann's parish and northeast Baltimore. These cakes are my absolute favorite. I must, however, admit my bias. Gertie was my grandmother and I grew up on these luscious spiced morsels of crab. This recipe has delighted four generations of my crab-loving family, so give them a try.

1 egg
2 tablespoons mayonnaise
1 teaspoon dry mustard
1/2 teaspoon ground black pepper
1 teaspoon Old Bay seasoning
2 teaspoons Worcestershire sauce

Dash of Tabasco sauce
1 pound lump or backfin crabmeat, picked over for shells
1/4 cup cracker crumbs
Vegetable oil for deep-frying

In a blender or mixing bowl, combine the egg, mayonnaise, mustard, pepper, Old Bay, Worcestershire sauce, and Tabasco sauce. Mix until frothy.

Place the crabmeat in a bowl, sprinkle on the cracker crumbs, and pour the egg mixture over the top. Gently toss or fold the ingredients together, taking care not to break up the lumps of crabmeat.

Form the cakes by hand or with an ice-cream scoop into rounded mounds about 3 inches in diameter and 1 inch thick. Do not pack the batter too firmly. The cakes should be as loose as possible, yet still hold their shape.

Pour oil into a deep skillet or a deep-fat fryer and heat to 375°F. Deep-fry the crab cakes, a few at a time, until golden brown on all sides, about 3 minutes. Remove to paper towels to drain briefly. Alternatively, slip the cakes under a preheated broiler, and broil, turning once, until nicely browned, about 3 minutes on each side.

Serve at once.

Faidley's World Famous Crab Cakes

Serves 4

The Faidley seafood stall, the Chesapeake-seafood centerpiece of Baltimore's Lexington Market, is the home of Charm City's most famous crab cake. Nancy and Bill Devine preside over the bustling family-run business. And when finally a free moment pre-

1 pound lump crabmeat, picked over for shells
1 cup crushed Saltines
1/2 cup mayonnaise
1 egg

1 tablespoon Dijon-style mustard
1 tablespoon Worcestershire sauce
Dash of Tabasco sauce
Vegetable oil for deep-frying

Spread the crabmeat out in a flat pan and sprinkle the crushed Saltines over the top.

In a small bowl mix together the mayonnaise, egg, mustard, Worcestershire sauce, and Tabasco sauce. Pour the mayonnaise over the crabmeat and

sents itself, Nancy dashes off to some European capital to act as Chesapeake ambassador and hostess at Baltimore-style crab feasts held for food aficionados on the Continent.

gently toss or fold the ingredients together, taking care not to break up the lumps of crabmeat. Let the mixture sit for 2 to 3 minutes before forming the cakes.

Form the mixture into mounded rounds about 3 inches in diameter and 1 inch thick. Do not pack the batter too firmly. The cakes should be as loose as possible, yet still hold their shape.

Pour oil into a deep skillet or a deep-fat fryer and heat to 375°F. Deep-fry the crab cakes, a few at a time, until golden brown on all sides, about 3 minutes. Remove to paper towels to drain briefly. Alternatively, to broil, slip the cakes under a preheated broiler and broil until nicely browned, about 5 to 6 minutes.

Serve at once.

Jenny's Cross Street Crab Cakes

Serves 4

Nick's Inner Harbor Seafood stall at Cross Street Market is a scene from turn-of-the-century Baltimore, with vendors hawking their wares and throngs of neighborhood residents enthusiastically doing their daily marketing. Behind the luncheon counter at Nick's stands Jenny Sours, who has been slinging her moist, delicious cakes "forever," or at least a decade. She is also known for her shrimp salad, seafood stew, and "fresh" tuna salad. She loves cooking all manner of seafood and tells me, hand on hip, cigarette dangling from her lips, "Hon, I'll fry anything that moves." So don't move too fast, but do try Miss Jenny's cakes. Umm good!

1 pound backfin crabmeat, picked over for shells
1 egg
1 tablespoon mayonnaise
2 teaspoons prepared mustard

2 teaspoons Old Bay seasoning
1 tablespoon Worcestershire sauce
1 tablespoon chopped fresh parsley
2 tablespoons cracker meal, or as needed

Place the crabmeat in a mixing bowl and set aside.

In a small bowl combine the egg, mayonnaise, mustard, Old Bay, Worcestershire sauce, and parsley. Mix well.

Sprinkle the cracker meal over the crabmeat and pour the egg mixture over the top. Gently toss or fold the ingredients together, taking care not to break up the lumps of crabmeat. If the batter seems too wet, add additional cracker meal.

Form the mixture into mounded rounds about 3 inches in diameter and 1 inch thick. Do not pack the batter too firmly. The cakes should be as loose as possible, yet still hold their shape.

Pour oil into a deep skillet or a deep-fat fryer and heat to 375°F. Deep-fry the crab cakes, a few at a time, until golden brown on all sides, about 3 minutes. Remove to paper towels to drain briefly. Alternatively, to broil, slip the cakes under a preheated broiler and broil until nicely browned, about 5 to 6 minutes.

Serve at once.

Company's Coming Crab Cakes

Serves 16 to 18

Miss Louise Watkins, of Severna Park, Maryland, swears by this recipe when she expects a crowd. Not only are these crab cakes delicious, but "this recipe'll stretch your pockeybook." For special occasions, such as Confirmations, First Communions, or the Fourth of July, she doubles or triples the recipe and mixes up her batches in an enamel washtub ("works better 'n mixin' bowls"). Louise serves these here cakes "family style," on a platter with overflowing bowls of potato salad, coleslaw, and a marinated cucumber-and-tomato salad.

2 pounds backfin or lump crabmeat, picked over for shells
2 pounds claw meat, picked over
   for shells
4 eggs
3/4 cup mayonnaise
1/4 cup finely minced yellow onion
   or green onion
4 teaspoons salt

2 teaspoons ground black pepper
4 teaspoons dry mustard
2 teaspoons paprika
1/4 cup fresh lemon juice
1/2 cup chopped fresh parsley
3 to 3 1/2 cups fine dried bread
   crumbs

In a large bowl mix together the two types of crabmeat. Set aside.

In a small bowl combine the eggs, mayonnaise, onion, salt, pepper, mustard, paprika, lemon juice, and parsley. Mix well.

Sprinkle the bread crumbs over the crabmeat and pour the egg mixture over the top. Gently toss or fold the ingredients together, taking care not to break up the lumps of crabmeat.

Form the mixture into mounded rounds about 3 inches in diameter and 1 inch thick. Do not pack the batter too firmly. The cakes should be as loose as possible, yet still hold their shape.

Pour oil into a deep skillet or a deep-fat fryer and heat to 375°F. Deep-fry the crab cakes, a few at a time, until golden brown on all sides, about 3 minutes. Remove to paper towels to drain briefly. Alternatively, to broil, slip the cakes under a preheated broiler and broil until nicely browned, about 5 to 6 minutes.

Serve at once.

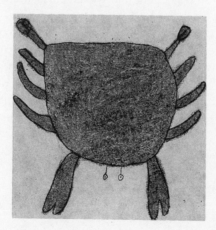

Kenny Opdyke
Kingsville Elementary School
Grade 5
Kingsville, Maryland

Crab Cakes "Ou La La"

Serves 4

Aunt Tina Martinelli, of Ruxton, Maryland, took a French cooking correspondence class and was binding up almost everything in sight with her newly discovered classic French sauces. She adapted an old family deviled crab recipe to arrive with this, her Crab Cakes "OU LA LA." The majority of Chesapeake-style crab cakes are mayonnaise based. This recipe, however, is bound by a tangy cream sauce and then lightly coated. It is a pleasant departure from tradition. When Tina serves these to guests, she accompanies them with scalloped potatoes and fresh asparagus topped with (but of course!) sauce hollandaise.

1 pound backfin or lump crabmeat, picked over for shells
2 tablespoons butter
2 tablespoons all-purpose flour
1/2 cup half-and-half or milk
1 egg yolk
1 tablespoon Dijon-style mustard
1 tablespoon prepared horseradish
1 tablespoon chopped drained capers
1/2 teaspoon salt
1/4 teaspoon ground black pepper
1/8 teaspoon ground cayenne pepper

Coating
2 eggs
1/2 cup milk
1/2 cup all-purpose flour
1 cup fine dried bread crumbs
Vegetable oil for frying

Place the crabmeat in a mixing bowl and set aside.

Melt the butter in a saucepan. Whisk in the flour and cook several minutes, stirring all the while.

Off the heat slowly whisk in the half-and-half or milk. Return the pan to the heat and whisk constantly until thick. Remove from the heat.

Whisk in the egg yolk, mustard, horseradish, capers, salt, black pepper, and cayenne pepper. Let the mixture cool for several minutes.

Pour the cream mixture over the crabmeat and gently mix together. Cover the mixture and chill in the refrigerator for at least 30 minutes before forming the cakes.

To prepare the coating, combine the eggs and milk in a bowl and beat until well mixed. Place the flour and bread crumbs in separate bowls.

Form the crab mixture into 8 cakes about 1 inch thick. Do not pack the batter too firmly. The cakes should be as loose as possible, but still hold their shape. Dust each cake lightly in flour, dip in the egg-milk mixture, and then coat well with bread crumbs. Chill at least 1 hour before frying.

In a large, heavy skillet, pour in oil until it reaches a depth of 1/2 inch. Add the cakes and panfry, turning several times, until golden brown, about 6 minutes' total cooking time.

Serve at once.

Crab Cakes Creole

Serves 4

Here are some zesty edibles for your crab cake edification. The prominent ingredients of an old southern-style Creole sauce infuse the crab cake batter, producing a refreshingly new kind of crab cake. The Remoulade Sauce, which follows, is a marvelous accompaniment for just about any cake recipe.

Remoulade Sauce (recipe follows)
1 pound backfin or lump crabmeat, picked over for shells
4 tablespoons butter
2 tablespoons finely diced yellow onion
1/4 cup minced green onion
1/2 small green bell pepper, seeded, deveined, and finely diced
1/2 small red bell pepper, seeded, deveined, and finely diced
1 egg
1 tablespoon mayonnaise

2 teaspoons Worcestershire sauce
1 tablespoon Creole-style mustard or any prepared hot mustard
1/2 teaspoon salt
1/4 teaspoon ground black pepper
1/8 teaspoon cayenne pepper
1/4 cup fine dried bread crumbs

Coating
1 egg
1/2 cup milk
1/2 cup all-purpose flour
1 cup fine dried bread crumbs

Prepare the sauce and chill for several hours.

Place the crabmeat in a mixing bowl and set aside.

In a saucepan melt the butter over medium-high heat. Add the yellow onion, green onion, and red and green bell peppers and sauté until soft, about 5 minutes. Put aside to cool to room temperature.

In a mixing bowl, combine the egg, mayonnaise, Worcestershire sauce, mustard, salt, black pepper, and cayenne pepper. Mix in the sautéed peppers.

Sprinkle the 1/4 cup bread crumbs over the crabmeat and pour the egg mixture over the top. Gently toss or fold the ingredients together, taking care not to break up the lumps of crabmeat. Form the mixture into 8 cakes about 1 inch thick. Do not pack the batter too firmly. The cakes should be as loose as possible, but still hold their shape.

To prepare the coating, combine the eggs and milk in a bowl and beat until well mixed. Place the flour and bread crumbs in separate bowls. Dust each cake lightly in the flour, dip in the egg-milk mixture, and then coat well with the bread crumbs. Chill cakes at least 1 hour before cooking.

Pour oil into a deep skillet or a deep-fat fryer and heat to 375°F. Deep-fry the crab cakes, a few at a time, until golden brown on all sides, about 3 minutes. Remove to paper towels to drain briefly.

Serve at once, with the sauce on the side.

Remoulade Sauce

Makes about 2 1/2 cups

1 cup mayonnaise

6 tablespoons finely minced celery

2 tablespoons finely minced green onions

1 tablespoon chopped fresh parsley

1 tablespoon minced garlic

2 tablespoons coarse-grain mustard

1 tablespoon Dijon-style mustard

2 tablespoons ketchup

2 tablespoons Worcestershire sauce

1 teaspoon Tabasco sauce

1 teaspoon paprika

1/4 teaspoon salt

In a bowl, mix together all the ingredients. Cover and chill several hours before serving.

Eastern Shore Crab Cakes

Serves 4

This is a recipe for pure, unadulterated crab cakes. The Eastern Shore of the Chesapeake is known for its deliciously simple version. The crabmeat is not overpowered by an array of seasonings but is allowed to shine through on its own.

1 pound backfin or lump crabmeat, picked over for shells

1 egg

1/4 pound butter, melted and cooled

2 tablespoons fresh lemon juice

1 tablespoon Worcestershire sauce

2 tablespoons chopped fresh parsley

3/4 to 1 cup fine dried bread crumbs

Vegetable oil for deep-frying, or clarified butter or olive oil, or a combination, for sautéing

Tartar Sauce (page 20)

Place the crabmeat in a mixing bowl and set aside.

In a small mixing bowl, combine the egg, butter, lemon juice, Worcestershire sauce, and parsley. Mix until frothy. Sprinkle crabmeat with bread crumbs and pour the egg mixture over the top. Gently toss or fold the ingredients together, taking care not to break up the lumps of crabmeat.

Form the mixture into mounded rounds about 3 inches in diameter and 1 inch thick. Do not pack the batter too firmly. The cakes should be as loose as possible, yet still hold their shape.

Pour oil into a deep skillet or a deep-fat fryer and heat to 375°F. Deep-fry the crab cakes, a few at a time, until golden brown on all sides, about 3 minutes. Remove to paper towels to drain briefly. Alternatively, to broil, slip the cakes under a preheated broiler and broil until nicely browned, about 5 to 6 minutes. Or heat a little clarified butter or olive oil, or a combination, in a skillet and sauté the cakes, turning several times, until golden brown, about 6 minutes' total cooking time.

Serve at once, with Tartar Sauce on the side.

Crab Cake Bennies

Serves 4

Bennies is brunch-cook lingo for multiple eggs Benedict orders. This is a variation on the traditional Benedict fare. Crab cakes, slightly flattened, replace the Canadian bacon. A brunch featuring this luxurious recipe is the perfect way to start a relaxing Sunday.

Crab cake recipe using 1 pound crabmeat
Hollandaise Sauce (recipe follows)

4 English muffins, fork split, lightly toasted, and buttered
8 eggs, poached

For the crab cake recipe, I recommend Gertie's Crab Cakes (page 30) or Eastern Shore Crab Cakes (page 35). Prepare the crab cake mixture as directed and form into 8 cakes that will fit on muffin halves. Prepare the sauce and keep warm.

Deep-fry or broil the cakes as directed in the recipe. Top each muffin half with a crab cake and then with a poached egg. Cover the eggs with warm sauce.

Hollandaise Sauce

Makes about 2 cups

8 egg yolks
1 tablespoon extra-dry vermouth
2 dashes of Tabasco sauce
2 dashes of Worcestershire sauce
Juice of 1 lemon

Pinch of salt
Pinch of ground white pepper
3/4 pound unsalted butter, melted and kept warm
Hot water, if needed

Place all the ingredients except for the butter and hot water in a heavy-bottomed stainless-steel saucepan. Whisk vigorously for 1 or 2 minutes.

Place the saucepan over low heat and whisk constantly until the yolks thicken, 1 or 2 minutes. Do not overcook or the eggs will scramble.

Remove the pan from the heat and slowly drizzle in the butter, whisking constantly to form a thick sauce. Keep the sauce warm for up to 15 minutes by placing it on a rack in a pot above simmering water. Whisk occasionally. If the sauce becomes too thick, or appears to be separating, whisk in a little hot water to thin.

Crod Cakes

Serves 8 to 10

This recipe appears to be a collaboration between a team of biogenetic engineers and a group of aquiculturists. The truth of the matter is, however, that when lunching with Miss Dolores Keh, the culinary wizard of Baltimore's Little Italy, I sampled her marvelous codfish cakes made with salt cod. Later, while playing around with her recipe (forgive me, Dolores), I blended in some crabmeat to see what would happen. The result is these tasty cod-and-crab cakes that, when served on a Saturday night with baked beans, will knock your socks right off.

1 pound boneless salt cod
4 tablespoons bacon drippings or butter
1 large onion, finely diced
2 cups riced or mashed cooked potatoes
1 pound claw crabmeat, picked over for shells
4 eggs, beaten
2 teaspoons Worcestershire sauce
1/2 teaspoon Tabasco sauce
1/4 cup chopped fresh dill or parsley
Juice of 1 lemon
Pinch of ground nutmeg
Freshly ground black pepper to taste
4 to 6 tablespoons butter or olive oil for sautéing cakes

Place the cod in a bowl, add water to cover, and refrigerate overnight, changing the water 2 or 3 times. Drain and flake into small bits. Set aside.

In a skillet, over medium-high heat, melt the bacon drippings or butter. Add the onion and sauté until soft, about 5 minutes.

In a large bowl, mix together the cod, onions, and potatoes. Add the crabmeat, eggs, Worcestershire, Tabasco, dill, lemon juice, nutmeg, and black pepper. Mix well.

Form the mixture into cakes about 1 inch thick. In a large skillet, over medium-high heat, melt the butter or heat the oil. Add the cakes and sauté, turning several times, until golden brown, about 6 minutes' total cooking time. Remove to paper towels to drain briefly.

Serve at once.

Black 'n' Blue Crab Cakes

Serves 8 as an entrée, or 16 to 20 as an appetizer

Susan Gunn, aka Susoise, a vivacious chef extraordinaire from Baltimore's Inner Harbor Sheraton Hotel, developed these mildly abused, but oh so scrumptious, crab cakes. The recipe is a truly fascinating blend of the traditional Chesapeake-style crab cake, the blackening method of New Orleans, and a fragrant haute cuisine butter sauce. Move over, Julia. Here comes Susoise!

Susan Gunn, saucier at the Sheraton Inner Harbor shown displaying the latest in crab fashionwear, is ready for a night on the town. Look out, Baltimore!

2 pounds lump crabmeat, picked
   over for shells
2 cups mayonnaise
1/2 cup sour cream
1/2 cup fresh lemon juice
1/2 cup Dijon-style mustard
2 tablespoons Old Bay seasoning
1 teaspoon Worcestershire sauce

1 teaspoon Tabasco sauce
2 tablespoons chopped fresh parsley
1 cup fine dried bread crumbs
Blackening Spice (recipe follows)
Clarified butter for sautéing
Reddened Butter Sauce (recipe
   follows)

Place the crabmeat in a large mixing bowl and set aside.

In a small bowl combine the mayonnaise, sour cream, lemon juice, mustard, Old Bay, Worcestershire sauce, Tabasco sauce, and parsley. Mix well.

Sprinkle the bread crumbs over the crabmeat and pour the mayonnaise mixture over the top. Gently toss or fold the ingredients together, taking care not to break up the lumps of crabmeat. Form the mixture into mounded rounds about 3 inches in diameter and 1 inch thick. Do not pack the batter too firmly. The cakes should be as loose as possible, yet still hold their shape.

Prepare the Blackening Spice and the Reddened Butter Sauce. Keep the sauce warm over very low heat.

Heat a large cast-iron skillet over high heat until smoking hot (the hotter the better). Dip each cake in clarified butter and roll in the spice. Cook for 2 to 3 minutes on each side.

Serve at once with the sauce.

NOTE: Whenever using this blackening method, be sure you are working in a well-ventilated area. This process produces a lot of smoke, so put on the exhaust fan and open the windows or the smoke alarms will be wailing.

Blackening Spice

Makes about 2 2/3 cups

1/2 cup paprika
1/2 cup Old Bay seasoning
1/4 cup cayenne pepper
1 tablespoon dried oregano
1 tablespoon dried basil

1 tablespoon dried whole thyme leaves
1 tablespoon onion powder
1 tablespoon garlic powder
1 teaspoon ground cumin
1 teaspoon ground black pepper

In a small bowl combine all the ingredients and mix well.

Reddened Butter Sauce

Makes about 1 1/2 cups

1 tablespoon olive oil
1 tablespoon minced onion
1 teaspoon minced garlic
Juice of 1 lemon
1/2 cup dry white wine
1 tablespoon tomato paste
2 cups heavy (whipping) cream

4 tablespoons butter, cut into small bits
1 teaspoon Blackening Spice (optional; recipe above)
1 teaspoon chopped fresh parsley
Salt and ground black pepper to taste

In a small saucepan over medium-high heat, warm the olive oil. Add the onion and garlic and sauté for 2 minutes. Add the lemon juice and wine. Bring to a boil and reduce slightly.

Whisk in the tomato paste and cream. Continue cooking until reduced by half. Add the blackening spice (if used), reduce the heat to low, and slowly whisk in the butter, piece by piece. Remove from the heat.

Add the parsley, salt, and pepper.

Calvert House Crab Cakes

Serves 4

For over a hundred years, the Calvert House of Baltimore has hosted generations of Baltimoreans and their guests. The Lutz family has operated the restaurant for the past twenty-six years. They are known far and wide for their crab specialties and also for their aged prime rib. Barbara Lutz always recommends their crab cakes to her customers, billing them as Baltimore's best. She backs up her claim with, "if you don't like them, you don't have to pay." She then adds, with a grin, that she's never had to give one away.

1 pound lump crabmeat, picked over for shells
2 eggs
3/4 cup mayonnaise
1/4 teaspoon dry mustard
1/8 teaspoon Old Bay seasoning

1 teaspoon chopped fresh parsley
4 slices white bread, crusts removed and bread diced
Clarified butter, or olive oil, or a combination, if sautéing

Preheat the broiler. Place the crabmeat in a mixing bowl and set aside.

In a small bowl, place the eggs, mayonnaise, dry mustard, Old Bay, and parsley. Mix well.

Scatter the bread on top of the crabmeat. Pour the egg mixture over the top. Gently toss or fold the ingredients together, taking care not to break up the lumps of crabmeat.

Form the mixture into mounded rounds about 3 inches in diameter and 1 inch thick. Do not pack the batter too firmly. The cakes should be as loose as possible, yet still hold their shape.

Slip the cakes under the broiler and broil until nicely browned. Alternatively, heat a little clarified butter or olive oil, or a combination, in a skillet and sauté the cakes, turning several times, until golden brown, about 6 minutes' total cooking time.

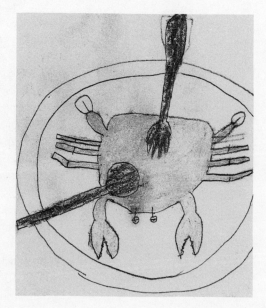

Jonathan Perry
Kingsville Elementary School
Grade 5
Kingsville, Maryland

Maryland Crab Cakes

Serves 4

Fifty years of research have sorted this recipe out as the best, according to Eastern Shore native Elbridge D. Tilghman, presently of Ocean City, Maryland. "There are probably hundreds of recipes to make the 'perfect' Maryland crab cake. I have tried making and have experienced eating countless varieties, including the famous Baltimore and Ohio Railroad dining car version, and two Crisfield, Maryland, restaurant versions, each one claiming to be the 'famous' one. I am now eight-four years of age and have concluded that this recipe is the best." So there you have it. Enjoy!

1 pound backfin crabmeat, picked over for shells
2 rounded tablespoons mayonnaise
1 tablespoon prepared mustard
3 tablespoons pancake mix (Bisquick is best)
1 egg
1/8 teaspoon Worcestershire sauce
2 tablespoons finely chopped fresh parsley
Fine dried bread crumbs and cracker crumbs for coating
Vegetable oil for frying

Place the crab meat in a mixing bowl and set aside.

In a small bowl combine the crabmeat, mustard, pancake mix, egg, Worcestershire sauce, and parsley. Mix well.

Pour the batter over the crabmeat. "Carefully mix, being careful not to break the lumps. I use a two-pronged kitchen fork. Use a serving spoon to make a cake form. Sprinkle with bread and cracker crumbs.

"Heat the oil in an iron skillet; it should be about 1/4 inch deep. When droplets of water splatter, place cakes in skillet. Fry until brown, about 2 minutes. Carefully turn and fry the other side about 1 minute. Remove and drain on paper towels."

· Appetizers and Salads ·

*Several of Baltimore's Gunning's Crab House crew are poised
and ready to serve up a pile of spicy, steamed blue crabs.
Pictured from left to right are Chris Alascio, Jackie Fereretti,
Cheryl Mullen, Sharon Willis, Ann Gunning, Charles Mowbray,
and Tammy Gunning.*

Crabmeat Pâté

Makes 1 pâté; serves 8 to 10

This crab pâté, which is bound together with sole, is an elegant centerpiece for any buffet table. For a more striking presentation bake the crab mixture in a fish-shaped mold instead of a loaf pan.

1/2 pound sole or flounder fillet
1 pound special crabmeat, picked
  over for shells
Juice of 1 lemon
1 teaspoon salt
1/4 teaspoon ground white pepper

2 eggs
1 1/2 cups heavy (whipping) cream
2 tablespoons chopped fresh dill
Boiling water, as needed
Dill Sauce (recipe follows)
Crackers or baguette slices

Preheat the oven to 350°F.

Cut the fish fillet into small pieces and place in a food processor. Add 1/2 pound of the crabmeat, the lemon juice, salt, and pepper. Process until the mixture is quite smooth.

Add the eggs and process well. With a rubber spatula scrape down any fish that has stuck to the sides of the processor bowl. With the machine running, slowly add the cream, and continue to process until completely incorporated. The mixture should be shiny and smooth.

Transfer the fish mixture to a mixing bowl and fold in the remaining 1/2 pound of crabmeat and the dill.

Butter a 6-cup terrine or loaf pan and pour in the pâté mixture. Place the mold in a baking pan and pour in boiling water to reach one-third of the way up the sides of the mold. Bake for 35 to 40 minutes, or until a knife inserted in the center of the pâté comes out clean.

Remove the pâté from the oven, cool to room temperature, cover, and refrigerate until well chilled. While the pâté is chilling, prepare the sauce and chill it as well.

To unmold the pâté run a wet knife around the edges of the pan. Invert the pâté onto a serving plate. Serve with crackers or baguette slices and the sauce on the side.

Dill Sauce

Makes about 1 1/2 cups

1 cup mayonnaise
1/2 cup sour cream
1 tablespoon chopped, drained
  capers

2 tablespoons chopped fresh dill
Pinch of ground white pepper

In a bowl, mix all the ingredients together well. Cover and chill for at least 1 hour prior to serving so that the flavors will blend.

Crabmeat Cocktail

Serves 4

Delectable pieces of lumb crab-meat and a pungent cocktail sauce are paired in this classic blue crab appetizer. It can be transformed into an exceptional salad by lightly dressing whole leaves of romaine with Remou-lade Sauce, mounding the crab-meat along the centers of the lettuce leaves, and then drizzling a thin line of sauce on top of the crabmeat.

1 small head romaine or iceberg lettuce, cut into very small pieces
1 pound lump crabmeat, picked over for shells

Cocktail Sauce (recipe follows) or Remoulade Sauce (page 35)
Lemon wedges and fresh parsley sprigs for garnish

In 4 cocktail glasses (actually I usually use ice-cream soda glasses), alternate layers of lettuce, crabmeat, and cocktail sauce, forming about 4 to 5 layers in all. Crown each cocktail with a big lump of meat resting on a dollop of sauce. Garnish with lemon wedges and parsley.

Cocktail Sauce

Makes about 2 1/2 cups

2 cups ketchup
1/2 cup prepared horseradish
1 tablespoon Worcestershire Sauce

1 teaspoon Tabasco sauce
Juice of 1 lemon

In a bowl combine all the ingredients and mix well.

Rolled Crabmeat Soufflé

Serves 6 to 8

Here is what you would concoct if a cookbook kept flipping be-tween a crab soufflé and a jelly roll. Voilà, a new creation—a crabmeat jelly roll! This recipe is actually inspired by a Simone Beck dish and is a wonderful first course for an elegant din-ner party. Whip up a batch of your best light tomato sauce to accompany it. Don't let the souf-flé preparation intimidate you. Once you've tried it, you'll find it's a piece of cake! Oh, no. Did that page flip again?

1 batch of your favorite imperial recipe (pages 69 to 71)
1/2 cup all-purpose flour
2 cups milk
4 egg yolks
1/2 teaspoon salt, plus pinch of salt

Freshly ground black pepper to taste
Freshly grated nutmeg to taste
6 egg whites
2/3 cup freshly shredded Swiss cheese

Prepare the imperial and place in the top section of a double boiler. Cover and heat gently. Preheat the oven to 375°F. Line a 9-by-13-inch baking sheet with aluminum foil. Butter and flour the foil, shaking out the excess flour.

Place the flour in a heavy-bottomed enamel or stainless-steel saucepan. Slowly add the milk, whisking constantly to form a smooth mixture. Place over medium heat and cook, stirring constantly, until thickened and smooth.

Remove the pan from the heat and beat in the yolks, one at a time. Add the 1/2 teaspoon salt, the pepper, and nutmeg. Set aside.

Place the egg whites and the pinch of salt in a bowl and, with an electric mixer, beat until stiff, but not dry. Fold the whites and cheese into the cream mixture; do not overmix.

Gently spread the mixture onto the prepared baking sheet. Bake until the soufflé rises and is nicely browned, about 20 minutes.

While the soufflé is baking, dampen (don't soak!) a large dish towel with warm water. Spread it out on a table or counter top. As soon as the soufflé is removed from the oven, invert the baking sheet onto the towel. Lift off the baking sheet and then peel off the foil. Whew!

Spread the warm imperial mixture evenly over the soufflé. Starting at a narrow end, carefully roll up the soufflé.

To serve, cut the soufflé crosswise into rounds, just as you would a jelly roll.

Juan Kelly's Crabmeat Tapas

Makes about 12 or so tartlets; serves 6 to 8, depending upon appetites

Señor Kelly, a part-time resident of Seville, Spain, a former Baltimore man-about-town, and most recently a deli owner in Berkeley, California, crafted this delightful Spanish-Chesapeake appetizer. Make sure to prepare plenty of these succulent morsels. At a cocktail party they disappear faster than "who-struck-Juan!"

12 prebaked Flaky Pastry Tartlet Shells (recipe follows)
1/4 cup olive oil
1 red bell pepper, seeded, deveined, and finely diced
1/2 cup mayonnaise
2 tablespoons minced drained capers
2 hard-cooked eggs, finely chopped
2 tablespoons minced yellow onion
Juice of 1/2 lemon
1/4 cup chopped fresh parsley
Freshly ground black pepper to taste
1 pound backfin or special crabmeat, picked over for shells
1/4 pound salted, air-dried ham such as Smithfield ham or prosciutto, cut into small dice
Green Spanish olives, pitted, for garnish

In a small skillet over medium-high heat, warm the olive oil. Add the bell pepper and sauté until soft, about 5 minutes. Put aside.

Bake the tartlet shells and let cool completely before filling.

In a large bowl mix together the mayonnaise, capers, eggs, onion, lemon juice, parsley, and black pepper.

Gently fold the crabmeat, ham, and sautéed peppers into the mayonnaise mixture. Mound the mixture into the prebaked tartlet shells and garnish with olives.

NOTE: If you don't have the time to make the tartlets, you may arrange the entire crab mixture in a pre-baked 12-inch tart shell.

Flaky Pastry Tartlet Shells

Makes about twelve to sixteen 2 1/2-inch tartlet shells

2 cups all-purpose flour
1/2 teaspoon salt
1/4 pound unsalted butter, cut into
very small pieces

2 tablespoons solid vegetable
shortening
3/4 cups ice water

Sift together the flour and salt into a mixing bowl. Work the butter and shortening into the flour with fingertips or a pastry blender until the mixture is the consistency of coarse meal.

Add the water, 1 tablespoon at a time, and mix with a fork after each addition. Dough should not be wet, but just moist enough to hold together. Form the dough into a ball. Wrap and refrigerate for at least 1 hour before using.

Preheat the oven to 425°F.

Divide the pastry into 4 equal portions. Work with 1 portion at a time and keep the others refrigerated.

On a lightly floured board, roll 1 portion of the dough into a round about 1/8 inch thick. With a round cookie cutter measuring 3 inches in diameter, cut out dough rounds. Transfer each round to a tartlet pan about 2 1/2 inches in diameter, pulling the dough gently to overlap the edges of the pan. Prick the bottoms with a fork. Line each pan with a small piece of aluminum foil pressed over the dough, or, better yet, stack another tartlet pan on top. Weight down with dried beans or raw rice.

Bake for 8 to 10 minutes. Remove foil or top pan and weights and bake uncovered until golden brown, about 1 minute.

Remove the pastry shells from the oven and let cool completely. Carefully remove the pastry shells from the pans.

Crackpot–Stuffed Mushroom Caps

Serves 8

When a group of Baltimore bartenders decided to open a seafood restaurant, one of their aunts proclaimed, "You're all a bunch of crackpots!" And thus was born the ever popular Crackpot Seafood Restaurant on the outskirts of Towson, Maryland. Here their talented seafood chef, Tom Lyons, who developed his culinary chops at the Crackpot, gives his recipe for the Pot's notoriously delicious stuffed mushroom caps.

1 egg white
1 teaspoon dry mustard
1 teaspoon Old Bay seasoning
3/4 cup mayonnaise
1 pound lump crabmeat, picked over for shells

1 pound medium-sized fresh mushrooms (about 24), stemmed
Imperial Sauce (recipe follows)
Paprika for garnish
Chopped fresh parsley for garnish

Preheat the oven to 350°F. In a medium bowl combine the egg white, mustard, Old Bay, and mayonnaise. Mix well. Gently fold the crabmeat into the mayonnaise mixture.

Stuff the mushroom caps with the crabmeat mixture, using approximately 1 heaping tablespoon for each cap. Place the stuffed caps, stuffing side up, on a baking sheet and cook until golden brown, 15 to 20 minutes.

While the mushrooms are baking, prepare the sauce.

Remove the mushrooms from the oven and top with sauce, using approximately 1 teaspoon of sauce per cap. Return to the oven until nicely browned, 3 to 5 minutes.

Remove the mushrooms from the oven and garnish with paprika and parsley. Serve at once.

Imperial Sauce

1 egg, beaten
2 cups mayonnaise
2 teaspoons Dijon-style mustard

1 teaspoon Old Bay seasoning
2 tablespoons dry sherry

In a small bowl combine all of the ingredients and mix well.

Sammy's Flying Crabmeat Saucers

Serves 6

Recipes linger on even after their creators pass away. And while preparing one of those treasured legacies of someone close to our hearts, it seems, through the smells, tastes, and textures, as if that person is still with us. Such is the case with these sand-wiches. My good friend, Sam Farace, was a gourmet's gour-met, known for his inspired food creations. So, while researching the "perfect" crab sandwich, I enlisted his help. With fond memories of cheese sandwiches his mom, El, made for him in a stove-top sandwich grill, Sammy created these scrumptious crabby saucers.

1/4 cup mayonnaise
2 teaspoons Dijon-style mustard
1 tablespoon chopped fresh dill
1 tablespoon chopped fresh parsley
Freshly ground black pepper
1 pound backfin or special crab-meat, picked over for shells

12 slices good-quality white bread
Softened butter
6 thin slices tomato (optional)
6 slices Cheddar, Swiss, or Havarti cheese

In a small bowl combine the mayonnaise, mustard, dill, parsley, and pepper. Mix well.

Place the crabmeat in a separate bowl and pour the dressing over the top. Mix gently.

To assemble the saucers, butter one side of each bread slice and place, butter side down, in a sandwich iron or electric sandwich maker. Put a generous spoonful of crab mixture in the middle of the bread. Cover the crab with a slice of tomato, if used, and a slice of cheese. Top with another bread slice, buttered side up. Close the sandwich iron and trim off excess bread with a knife. Cook until golden brown on both sides.

Cooked saucers may be held in a warm oven while other saucers are being prepared and launched.

Jo-Jo's Curried Crustacean Dip

Serves 8 or so

Ms. Joanne Turner-Slemp loves a party. She found her old run-of-the-mill crab dip fine for every day, but not quite having the pizzazz she needed for her infa-mous Bay-side bashes. Well, she's gone and done it with this curry-infused dip that will set your hips to shaking and your feet to dancing, not to mention your mouth a-watering!

1/2 cup dried currants
Boiling water, as needed
1 pound cream cheese, softened
1 tablespoon Madras curry powder
2 tablespoons mayonnaise

1/4 cup coconut milk or heavy (whipping) cream
1/4 cup minced green onion
1 pound special or claw crabmeat, picked over for shells
Melba rounds

Preheat the oven to 350°F.

In a small bowl place the currants and just enough boiling water to cover. Let stand for 10 minutes. Drain, reserving the liquid, and put currants aside.

In a large bowl combine the cream cheese, curry powder, mayonnaise, coconut milk or cream, and green onion. Whisk until smooth and creamy. Mix in the crabmeat, currants, and reserved currant liquid.

Transfer the crab mixture to a small casserole dish. Bake for 25 to 30 minutes. Serve hot or warm with Melba rounds.

Ginger's Crabmeat Supreme Pastries

Serves 6

Ginger Silvers, a gracious Washington, D.C., food columnist, cookbook author, and cooking instructor, came up with these magnificent crabmeat appetizers. They are guaranteed to wow any cocktail party crowd.

1 pound backfin crabmeat, picked over for shells
1/2 cup chopped celery
1/4 cup chopped fresh parsley
3/4 cup mayonnaise
1/8 teaspoon Tabasco sauce

1/4 teaspoon Worcestershire sauce
Salt to taste
One 10-ounce package frozen patty shells (6 shells), thawed in the package in the refrigerator
Pimiento Sauce (recipe follows)

Preheat the oven to 425°F.

In a bowl combine the crabmeat, celery, parsley, mayonnaise, Tabasco sauce, Worcestershire sauce, and salt.

On a lightly floured board, roll out each patty shell into a round. Spoon about 1/3 cup crabmeat mixture into the center of each; fold up ends to enclose the filling completely. Place the pastries, sealed ends down, on an ungreased baking sheet. (At this point you may refrigerate the pastries for 4 to 6 hours.)

Bake the pastries until nicely browned, 35 to 45 minutes. Meanwhile, prepare the sauce.

Serve the pastries at once with the sauce.

Pimiento Sauce

Makes about 2 cups

4 tablespoons butter
1/4 cup all-purpose flour
2 1/2 cups milk
1/2 teaspoon salt
1/8 teaspoon ground white pepper

1 teaspoon finely minced onion
1 teaspoon freshly grated lemon or orange peel
1/2 cup chopped pimientos

In a saucepan melt the butter over medium heat. Whisk in the flour and cook, stirring constantly, for 2 to 3 minutes. Take care not to brown the flour.

Off the heat slowly whisk in the milk. Add the salt, pepper, onion, and lemon peel. Return to low heat and cook, stirring constantly, until thickened. Stir in the pimientos.

This sauce may be prepared 1 day in advance and refrigerated. Reheat in a double boiler.

Working crab pots near the Eastern Shore of the Chesapeake Bay, Captain Gary Phillips guides his boat, the Pamela Lynn II, toward another pot as Brian Lowery empties blue crabs into a holding bin.

Susan's Crab Meltaways

Serves 12

Ms. Susan Corsaro is a seeker. She dabbles in metaphysics with entities both near and far from the Chesapeake. She is, nevertheless, a no-nonsense gal. At a touchy-feely encounter group, a fellow seeker was a bit overzealously euphoric with an on-premise entity when Susan, suspiciously eyeing him up and down, leaned over to him and admonished, "Hon, get a grip!" Here's Susan's tasteful, easy-to-prepare party or light luncheon dish that you and your guests can get a grip on, too.

12 ounces sharp Cheddar cheese, shredded
1/4 cup mayonnaise
1/4 pound butter
2 tablespoons Old Bay seasoning

1 teaspoon minced garlic
1 cup chopped fresh parsley
1 pound special or claw crabmeat, picked over for shells
12 English muffins, fork split

In the top pan of a double boiler, place the cheese, mayonnaise, butter, Old Bay, and garlic. Heat slowly, stirring occasionally, until the cheese is completely melted. Stir in the parsley and crabmeat.

Arrange the muffin halves on an ungreased baking sheet and divide the crabmeat mixture among them, spreading it on evenly. Cover and freeze for at least 2 hours. Preheat the oven to 425°F. Move the baking sheet from the freezer to the oven and bake until nicely browned, 15 to 20 minutes.

The muffin halves can be served whole or cut into quarters for hors d'oeuvres.

Thelma's Crab and Artichoke Dip

Serves 8 to 10

This rich and satisfying dip recipe from Baltimore's Thelma Tunney is actually prepared like a casserole. It teams blue crabmeat with tender artichoke hearts in a lightly spiced mayonnaise-based sauce. It not only works well as a party dip served with crusty baguette slices or crackers but also makes an excellent entrée accompanied with toast points.

8 ounces sharp Cheddar cheese, shredded
2 cups mayonnaise
1 tablespoon Dijon-style mustard
2 teaspoons Worcestershire sauce
1/8 teaspoon cayenne pepper
Juice of 1 lemon

Freshly ground black pepper
One 16-ounce jar artichoke hearts, drained and cut into small pieces
1 pound backfin or special crabmeat, picked over for shells
1/2 cup chopped fresh parsley

Preheat the oven to 350°F. Butter a 6-cup casserole dish.

In a large bowl combine the cheese, mayonnaise, mustard, Worcestershire sauce, cayenne pepper, lemon juice, and black pepper. Stir until well mixed. Gently fold in the artichoke hearts, crabmeat, and parsley.

Pour the crabmeat mixture into the dish and bake for 20 to 25 minutes. Serve at once.

Miss Alice's Crab Fluffs

Serves 8 to 10

The Harrisons of Tilghman Island are one of the Chesapeake's first families of seafood. Matriarch Alice Harrison presides over their charming Eastern Shore hotel and restaurant in St. Michaels, Maryland, where part of the Chesapeake's legendary skipjack fleet is docked. Miss Alice's light-as-air crab fluffs, mounds of delicately spiced crab lumps coated with an aromatic batter, are Eastern Shore cookery at its finest.

Alice Harrison, of Harrison's Country Inn and Chesapeake House, is one of the first ladies of Eastern Shore cooking. For years she has been entertaining her guests with some of the finest Chesapeake fare to be found.

Tartar Sauce (page 20) or
    Remoulade Sauce (page 35)
1 pound backfin or claw crabmeat,
    picked over for shells
1 egg
1/3 cup mayonnaise
1 teaspoon Worcestershire sauce
1 teaspoon dry mustard
1/2 teaspoon salt
1/4 teaspoon ground black pepper
1/2 cup fine dried Italian bread
    crumbs

Batter
1 1/2 cups all-purpose flour
2 teaspoons baking powder
1 teaspoon Old Bay seasoning
1/2 teaspoon salt
1/4 teaspoon celery seed
1/4 teaspoon lemon-pepper
    seasoning
2 eggs, beaten
2 tablespoons mayonnaise
1/4 teaspoon prepared mustard
1 cup milk
Vegetable oil for deep-frying

Prepare the sauce and chill well. Place the crabmeat in a bowl and set aside.

In a mixing bowl combine the egg, mayonnaise, Worcestershire, dry mustard, salt, and pepper. Mix well.

Pour the egg mixture over the crabmeat and sprinkle the bread crumbs over all. Gently mix or fold the ingredients together. Form into little balls about 1 1/2 inches in diameter. Refrigerate until ready to cook.

To prepare the batter sift the flour and baking powder together into a mixing bowl. Combine all of the remaining ingredients and whisk together to make a smooth batter.

Pour oil into a deep skillet or a deep-fat fryer and heat to 375°F. Coat the balls with the batter and deep-fry, a few at a time, until golden brown. Remove to paper towels to drain briefly.

Serve at once with Tartar Sauce or Remoulade Sauce.

Back Creek Inn's Crab Quiche

Serves 6 to 8

On the tree-lined banks of Back Creek, one of southern Maryland's scenic waterways, sits Carol Szkotnicki and Lin Cochran's charming Back Creek Inn. This superb crab quiche is served to their fortunate summer guests who often help the proprietors catch crabs from the inn's pier. Use your best savory pie crust recipe as a cradle for this fine Maryland dish.

Lin Cochran, left, and Carol Szkotnicki are the proprietors of the charming Back Creek Inn in southern Maryland. Here their guests can lie back and enjoy the area's serene atmosphere, or perhaps try their hand at crabbing with pots off the Inn's pier.

One 9-inch unbaked pie shell
3 eggs, lightly beaten
1/2 cup mayonnaise
2 tablespoons all-purpose flour
1 teaspoon chopped fresh thyme
Freshly ground black pepper

8 ounces Swiss cheese, finely shredded
1/2 small onion, thinly sliced
1 pound backfin or special crab-meat, picked over for shells
Fresh thyme sprigs and sliced fresh fruit for garnish

Prepare the pie shell and set aside. Preheat the oven to 350°F.

In a bowl combine the eggs, mayonnaise, flour, thyme, and black pepper. Mix well. Gently stir in the cheese, onion, and crabmeat.

Pour the crab mixture into the pie shell. Bake until a knife inserted in the center comes out clean, about 40 minutes.

Garnish each serving with a thyme sprig and sliced fresh fruit.

William Taylor's Marinated Crab Salad with Raspberries

Serves 4 to 5

Bill Taylor, the exuberant Dinner Designer of Nat Creek in southern Maryland, is Hollywood's (Maryland, not California) host with the most. His theme cooking classes and historically in-tune plantation dinner parties are the talk of the town. This exquisitely balanced crab salad is the epitome of summer fare on the Chesapeake.

Southern Maryland's effervescent dinner designer, William C. Taylor, pauses in front of a mural at the National Aquarium in Baltimore during the preparations for one of his celebrated cooking classes and dinners.

1 pound lump or backfin crabmeat, picked over for shells
4 tablespoons raspberry vinegar
1 heaping tablespoon drained capers
1/2 cup mayonnaise
Juice of 1 lime

Dash of cayenne pepper
1 large cucumber
2 teaspoons sugar
Boston lettuce leaves
Fresh raspberries for garnish
Lime slices for garnish

Place the crabmeat in a shallow bowl and sprinkle 2 tablespoons of the raspberry vinegar over the top. Transfer the crabmeat to a colander and add the capers. Toss gently to mix and to allow excess vinegar to drain off.

Place the crabmeat and capers in a bowl. Gently fold in the mayonnaise to bind the lumps together. Cover and chill. Just before serving squeeze in the fresh lime juice and add a good dash of cayenne; mix gently.

Slice the unpeeled cucumber as thinly as possible or shred it. Sprinkle with the remaining 2 tablespoons raspberry vinegar and the sugar. Mix well.

Serve the salad on a large plate or on individual plates. Mound the crab mixture on the lettuce leaves. Surround with the cucumber mixture and garnish with the raspberries. Top with lime slices. Serve quite cold.

Crab Louie

Serves 4

My great-aunt Minnie moved out to San Francisco and was there during the 1906 earthquake. That was enough for her. She

Louis Dressing (recipe follows)
Shredded lettuce
1 pound lump crabmeat, picked over for shells

4 hard-cooked eggs, quartered
2 ripe tomatoes, cored and quartered

Prepare the dressing and chill well.

packed what china survived and headed back to the Chesapeake. She also brought back with her this West Coast treatment for Dungeness crab. Minnie knew that using the blue crabmeat of her home turf would be a hit, and she was right!

Make a bed of lettuce on a large serving platter. Carefully arrange the crabmeat atop the lettuce. Garnish with the eggs and tomatoes. Pour the dressing over all.

Louis Dressing

Makes about 1 3/4 cups

1 cup mayonnaise
2 tablespoons grated onion
1/2 teaspoon minced garlic
1/4 cup canned tomato sauce

1/4 cup chopped fresh parsley
Dash of Tabasco sauce
Pinch of cayenne pepper
1/3 cup heavy (whipping) cream

In a small bowl combine the mayonnaise, onion, garlic, tomato sauce, parsley, Tabasco sauce, and cayenne pepper. Mix well.

Lightly whip the cream. Gently fold the cream into the mayonnaise. Cover and refrigerate for at least 1 hour before serving.

Eastern Shore Crab Salad with Melon

Serves 6

The soil of the Chesapeake's Eastern Shore produces some of the sweetest, most fragrant summer melons imaginable. This refreshing salad is the perfect dish for a relaxing patio luncheon cooled by honeysuckle-scented breezes.

1 pound backfin crabmeat, picked over for shells
1/4 cup diced red bell pepper
1/4 cup diced green bell pepper
2 tablespoons minced green onion
1/4 cup diced apple
3/4 cup mayonnaise
1/4 cup sour cream
1 tablespoon honey

2 tablespoons chopped fresh mint
Dash of Worcestershire sauce
Dash of Tabasco sauce
Juice of 1/2 lemon
Salt and ground black pepper to taste
3 small ripe cantaloupe or honeydew melons, halved and seeded
Whole fresh mint sprigs for garnish

In a large bowl combine the crabmeat, red and green bell peppers, onion, and apple.

In a small bowl combine the mayonnaise, sour cream, honey, chopped mint, Worcestershire sauce, Tabasco sauce, and lemon juice. Mix well. Pour the mayonnaise mixture over the crabmeat mixture and toss gently. Season with salt and pepper.

Place each melon half, cut side up, on an individual salad plate. Divide the salad mixture evenly among the melon halves, mounding the salad in the hollow centers. Garnish with the mint sprigs.

· Soups and Chowders ·

Geraldine Davis, gospel singer and down-home Chesapeake
cook, puts on some pearls and takes a break—while
possibly dreaming up some inspired dishes
to delight her family and friends.

Miss Geraldine's Old-Fashioned Country Crab Soup

Serves a crowd

Miss Geraldine Davis—gospel singer over to the Freedom Tabernacle Holiness Church, actress, beauty technician with Sartori's 2000 Hair Salon in the Mount Washington area of Baltimore, Maryland, and down-home cook—serves up food so inspiring it just might make you jump up and shout. Miss Geraldine loves summer cooking, "just puttin' this and that in the pot and coming up with 'something.' Honey, that's what cookin's all about!" Geraldine serves her soup with plenty of hot corn bread to "dunk in the bowl so you can sop up the juice." This is one of my all-time favorite crab soups.

4 quarts water
Two 28-ounce cans peeled whole tomatoes
One 6-ounce can tomato paste
2 bay leaves
1/2 cup chopped fresh parsley
2 tablespoons Old Bay seasoning
4 stalks celery, diced
1 large onion, chopped
1 smoked neckbone (about 3 pounds)
1 small beef bone
Salt and ground black pepper to taste
2 tablespoons Worcestershire sauce
8 live soup crabs (see Note), cleaned and quartered, with top shells reserved (page 11)

1 small head cabbage, finely chopped
4 medium potatoes, cut into 1/2-inch dice
1 cup diced carrots (1/4-inch dice)
1 cup cut-up green beans (1/2-inch lengths)
1 cup freshly cut corn kernels
1 cup fresh or frozen green peas
1 cup fresh or frozen lima beans
1 cup diced green bell pepper (1/4-inch dice)
2 pounds claw crabmeat, picked over for shells

In a large soup pot, combine the water, tomatoes, tomato paste, bay leaves, parsley, Old Bay, celery, onion, smoked neck, beef bone, salt, black pepper, and Worcestershire sauce. Bring to a boil.

Simmer gently uncovered for 1 hour, then add the soup crabs with their top shells. Continue cooking for another 30 minutes. Add the cabbage, potatoes, carrots, green beans, corn, peas, lima beans, and bell pepper. Simmer until the vegetables are tender, about 30 minutes. Add the claw meat and simmer a little longer, 20 to 25 minutes.

Discard the crab top shells. Serve the soup in deep bowls.

NOTE: Soup crabs are whole male or female blue crabs that are too small for steaming.

Bo Brook's E-Z Maryland Crab Soup

Serves 4 to 6

Paul Storke, the affable manager of Bo Brook's Crab House, one of Baltimore's premier crab establishments, provides a no-muss-no-fuss-fifty-minute crab soup for you gourmets on the go. And it's right tasty to boot!

4 cups water
One 8-ounce can crushed tomatoes
2 beef bouillon cubes
2 tablespoons Old Bay seasoning
1 teaspoon ground black pepper
1 small onion, chopped

4 stalks celery, chopped
1/2 small head cabbage, cored and sliced
1 pound claw crabmeat, picked over for shells

In a soup pot combine the water, tomatoes, bouillon cubes, Old Bay, and pepper. Bring to a boil. Add the onion, celery, and cabbage and simmer uncovered for 20 minutes.

Add the crabmeat and continue cooking for 10 minutes more.

NOTE: If you're not in a hurry, make this soup a day ahead and refrigerate overnight. It has an even better flavor when it is reheated.

Pauleen's Blue Crab Gumbo

Serves a crowd

Mumbo jumbo who's got the gumbo? Well, Miss Pauleen Lee, down southern Maryland way does, and it's a pot-au-many ingredients she's brewing that'll set a grown man's eyes to tearin' and lips to smackin'. She confides, "Darlin', it's all in the roux. Don't want it lookin' like oatmeal and don't want it burnt to the devil. Gotta be the color of a rusty old nail." In case you're fresh out of rusty nails, the shade you're aiming for is a dark reddish brown. The roux not only thickens the gumbo and gives it its color, but it also imparts a distinctive nutty flavor to the dish.

3/4 cup vegetable oil
3/4 cup bacon drippings or rendered chicken fat
1 1/2 cups all-purpose flour
2 large onions, diced (1/4-inch dice)
2 cups diced celery (1/4-inch dice)
2 green bell peppers, seeded, deveined, and cut into 1/4-inch dice
2 cups finely chopped green onions
3 tablespoons minced garlic
4 cups chopped, peeled ripe fresh tomatoes, or two 16-ounce cans diced tomatoes
16 live soup crabs (see Note), cleaned and halved (page 11)

2 quarts water
2 teaspoons salt
1 teaspoon ground black pepper
1 teaspoon dried thyme
1 teaspoon dried basil
1 teaspoon dried oregano
1 bay leaf
1/2 teaspoon cayenne pepper
1 teaspoon Tabasco sauce
1 pound okra, cut into pieces
1 pound shrimp, peeled and deveined
1 pound special or claw crabmeat, picked over for shells
Filé powder to taste

In a heavy-bottomed soup pot, heat the oil and bacon drippings or chicken fat until just about smoking hot. Whisk in the flour and stir constantly over medium-high heat until the mixture turns a dark reddish brown, about 5 minutes. Keep whisking the roux or it will burn and stick to the bottom. Be careful not to splash it on your skin!

Cook up a big pot of fluffy white rice while the gumbo is simmering. Serve the gumbo ladled over the rice and pass plenty of hot corn bread.

When roux is properly browned, turn off the heat and stir in the onions, celery, bell peppers, green onions, and garlic. Return to medium heat and cook, stirring all the while, until soft and browned, about 6 to 8 minutes.

Add the tomatoes, soup crabs, water, salt, black pepper, thyme, basil, oregano, bay leaf, cayenne pepper, and Tabasco sauce. Bring to a boil, reduce the heat, and simmer uncovered for 1 hour.

Stir in the okra and simmer for 30 minutes more. Add the shrimp and crabmeat and continue to simmer for 30 minutes. Just before serving add filé to taste.

NOTE: Soup crabs are whole male or female blue crabs that are too small for steaming.

Leigh's Cream of Crab Soup

Serves 8 to 10

Ms. Debra Botterill of McCormick's Old Bay seasoning division—you know, the Chesapeake's ubiquitous seafood spice—provided this recipe from their collection of treasured recipes. It is a tasteful soup that has a perfectly seasoned base and allows the crab to shine through.

Around the Chesapeake, Old Bay Seasoning is virtually synonymous with crabs. Its distinctive flavor and pungent aroma have been tantalizing the locals for generations.

6 tablespoons butter
1 small onion, finely diced
2 small potatoes, peeled and cut into medium dice
2 teaspoons Old Bay seasoning
1 tablespoon dry mustard
1/4 cup all-purpose flour
1 teaspoon salt
1/4 teaspoon ground black pepper
4 cups half-and-half
2 cups milk
1 pound backfin or special crabmeat, picked over for shells
2 tablespoons dry sherry
2 tablespoons chopped parsley

In a heavy-bottomed soup pot, melt the butter over medium-high heat. Add the onion and sauté for 2 to 3 minutes. Add the potatoes, Old Bay, and mustard. Reduce the heat to low and cook, stirring often, until the potatoes are just barely tender, about 30 minutes.

Remove from the heat and whisk in the flour, salt, and pepper. Return to medium heat and stir constantly for 2 minutes.

Slowly pour in the half-and-half and milk, stirring constantly. Cook over medium-low heat, stirring often, until thickened. Add the crabmeat and simmer for an additional 15 to 20 minutes.

When ready to serve, stir in the sherry and parsley.

Virginia She-Crab Soup

Serves 6

There is no other seafood soup more closely associated with the Old South than this roe-laden cream of crab soup. Pass around some additional dry sherry so that your guests may add a touch to their bowls of steaming soup.

12 live female blue crabs (sooks)
8 tablespoons (1/4 pound) butter
1 small onion, finely diced
3 tablespoons all-purpose flour
2 cups Fish Stock (recipe follows)
2 cups heavy (whipping) cream
1 teaspoon Worcestershire sauce
1/4 teaspoon Tabasco sauce

1 teaspoon salt
Ground white pepper to taste
1/4 cup dry sherry
1 tablespoon minced shallot
1/2 cup heavy (whipping) cream,
  lightly whipped, for garnish
Cayenne pepper for garnish

In a steamer pot or large, heavy pot with a tight-fitting lid, pour in water to a depth of 2 to 3 inches. Put a round raised rack into the pot that is tall enough to clear the liquid. Bring to a good strong boil.

Place the crabs on the rack, cover, and steam over moderately high heat until the crabs are bright red, about 20 minutes. Remove the crabs from the rack and, when cool enough to handle, pick out the meat and orange-colored roe. Set aside.

In a heavy-bottomed pot, melt 4 tablespoons of the butter over medium heat, add the onion, and sauté until tender, about 5 minutes. Whisk in the flour and cook over medium heat, stirring constantly, 2 to 3 minutes. Take care not to brown the mixture.

Off the heat slowly whisk in the stock and cream. Add the Worcestershire sauce and Tabasco sauce. Return the pot to medium heat and stir frequently until the mixture thickens, about 20 minutes. Add the salt, pepper, and sherry. Simmer for 20 to 25 minutes.

Nora Grunner, a native Baltimorean, moved to Fairbanks, Alaska, to work as a newspaper photographer. A recent trip home brought her to a long-awaited table of steamed crabs and beer. Here Nora poses for some crab hijinx at Gunning's Crab House.

In a sauté pan heat the remaining 4 tablespoons butter over medium-high heat. Add the shallot and sauté for about 1 minute. Add the reserved crabmeat and roe. Heat for 1 to 2 minutes, tossing the crabmeat in the butter to coat evenly. Add the crabmeat mixture to the soup and reheat for several minutes.

Ladle into soup bowls and top with whipped cream and a light sprinkling of cayenne pepper.

Fish Stock

Makes about 7 cups

This recipe makes more stock than is needed for the previous recipe; freeze the remainder to have on hand for use in other recipes.

3 1/2 to 4 pounds fish heads, bones, or trimmings
8 cups water
2 onions, sliced
3 stalks celery, chopped
2 carrots, peeled and chopped

4 cloves garlic, unpeeled
2 bay leaves
1 tablespoon whole black peppercorns
2 teaspoons whole dried thyme
1/2 bunch fresh parsley

In a large pot combine all the ingredients and bring to a boil. Reduce the heat to medium and simmer uncovered for 30 minutes. Skim the foam from the top often.

Strain the stock through a fine sieve or cheesecloth.

Gunning's Cream of Crab Soup

Serves 5 or 6

Before the diners at Baltimore's famous Gunning's Crab House go to town with piles of spicy steamed blue crabs, they most often whet their appetites with this pleasantly simple cream of crab soup. Owner Ed Gunning and manager Calvin Etheridge tell me that their loyal customers suck up this soup almost faster than they can make it. Try a bowl for yourself and you'll understand why.

1/4 pound butter
3/4 cup cornstarch
2 cups water
One 12-ounce can cream of celery soup, undiluted
4 cups milk

1 pound backfin, special, or claw crabmeat, picked over for shells
Salt and ground white pepper to taste
Minced fresh chives or green onions for garnish (optional)

In a heavy-bottomed pot, melt the butter over medium heat. Meanwhile, in a small bowl whisk the cornstarch and water together. Stir the cornstarch mixture into the butter. Add the celery soup, milk, and crabmeat. Cook over medium heat, stirring constantly, until thickened. Season with salt and pepper.

Serve garnished with chives or green onions, if desired.

NOTE: For a spicier soup add a dash each of Worcestershire sauce and Tabasco sauce with the salt and pepper.

Norfolk Crab Chowder

Serves 8 to 10

A hearty, full-flavored chowder that brings together two of Norfolk's most highly prized delicacies, cured Smithfield ham and Chesapeake blue crab, an unparalleled couple.

1/4 pound salt pork, finely diced
2 tablespoons butter
1/4 pound Smithfield ham, finely diced
1 medium onion, diced (1/4-inch dice)
1 cup diced celery (1/4-inch dice)
1 small green bell pepper, seeded, deveined, and cut into 1/4-inch dice
1 small red bell pepper, seeded, deveined, and cut into 1/4-inch dice
2 tablespoons minced garlic
3 cups Fish Stock (page 61) or clam juice
6 live blue crabs, cleaned and halved, with top shells reserved (page 11)

4 cups diced peeled potatoes (1/2-inch dice)
1/2 teaspoon dried thyme
1/4 teaspoon cayenne pepper
1/2 teaspoon Tabasco sauce
2 tablespoons Worcestershire sauce
1 bay leaf
3 cups half-and-half or heavy (whipping) cream
2 cups freshly cut corn kernels
1 pound claw crabmeat, picked over for shells
Salt and freshly ground black pepper to taste
Chopped fresh parsley for garnish
Chowder or oyster crackers

In a heavy-bottomed pot, over medium-high heat, fry the salt pork until the fat is rendered and the salt pork is crisp and brown. With a slotted spoon, remove the bits of browned salt pork and discard. Add the butter to the pot and melt over medium heat. Add the ham and cook for about 2 minutes. Add the onion, celery, red and green bell peppers, and garlic and sauté for 2 to 3 minutes.

Add the stock, crabs, top shells, potatoes, thyme, cayenne pepper, Tabasco sauce, Worcestershire sauce, bay leaf, and half-and-half or cream. Cook until the potatoes are just tender, 20 to 30 minutes. Add the corn and continue cooking for another 15 minutes.

Remove the top shells from the chowder and discard. Add the crabmeat and heat through. Garnish with chopped parsley and serve with crackers.

Ed's Rockfish, Crab, and Corn Chowder

Serves 8 to 10

Chef Ed Keene of Charm City (Baltimore, that is) brought his childhood memories into play when he created this inspired chowder. Every summer Ed's family would fish and crab near the Chesapeake Bay Bridge. The resulting catch would always include a bushel of crabs and a rockfish or two. On the drive back to the city they would stop by one of the many roadside farmers' produce stalls and buy deliciously sweet Silver Queen corn. Once home the clan would have their fill of crabs, fish, and corn. The leftovers produced this family culinary treasure.

Stock
One 4- to 6-pound rockfish, cleaned and filleted, bones and head reserved
2 carrots, peeled and chopped
1 onion, studded with 3 whole cloves stuck through 1 bay leaf
1 bunch fresh parsley stems
1 tablespoon dried whole thyme leaves

Chowder
6 ears Silver Queen corn
4 tablespoons sweet butter

1 large onion, cut into 1/4-inch dice
3 medium potatoes, cut into 1/4-inch dice
1/4 cup flour
2 cups heavy (whipping) cream
1 pound backfin crabmeat, picked over for shells
2 tablespoons chopped fresh parsley
Salt and ground black pepper to taste

To make the stock, place the fish head and bones in an 8-quart stockpot and add water to cover. Reserve the fish fillets for later use. Add the carrots, onion, parsley stems, and thyme. Bring to a boil, reduce the heat to low, and simmer for 2 hours, uncovered. Skim the foam from the top occasionally. Strain the stock through a fine strainer before adding it to the chowder.

Once the stock is simmering, begin making the chowder. Husk the corn and cut the kernels off the ears with a sharp knife, collecting the kernels and any "corn milk" in a bowl. Put kernels and corn milk aside. Add the corn cobs to the simmering stock.

In a large, heavy-bottomed pot, melt 2 tablespoons of the butter. Add the onions and sauté until translucent, 3 to 5 minutes. Add the potatoes and continue sautéing for 4 to 5 minutes. Stir in the flour and cook, stirring constantly, for 2 to 3 minutes. Stir in the strained stock and bring to a boil. Reduce heat until the chowder is at a simmer.

Cut the rockfish fillets into 3/4-inch cubes. Add the cubes to the chowder along with corn and corn milk. Stir in the cream. Add the crabmeat and simmer, stirring occasionally, 45 minutes to 1 hour.

Just before serving, add the parsley and the remaining 2 tablespoons of butter. Season with salt and pepper. Serve piping hot.

Crab Chili

Serves 8

Who needs a ground beef chili when there's plenty of crabs around! This south-of-the-border, seafood stewish–style chili is so good you'll never want chili any other way. If crabs are out of season, this dish works well with shrimp, firm-fleshed fish fillets, squid, and on and on. Serve with corn bread or biscuits. Be careful. This chili packs a punch!

1/4 cup olive oil
2 cups diced onion (1/4-inch dice)
2 tablespoons minced garlic
1 teaspoon hot-pepper flakes
1/4 teaspoon cayenne pepper
2 teaspoons ground cumin
4 teaspoons chili powder
2 tomatillos, papery husks removed, cored, and finely chopped
4 cups fresh or canned chopped, peeled tomatoes
3 cups Fish Stock (page 61)
1 teaspoon dried oregano
1 bay leaf
1 teaspoon salt
3/4 cup masa harina (see Note)
2 cups cooked black beans
1 pound claw crabmeat, picked over for shells
Sour cream for garnish

In a large, heavy-bottomed pot, heat the olive oil over medium-high heat. Add the onion, garlic, and pepper flakes and sauté for 5 minutes. Add the cayenne, cumin, chili powder, tomatillos, tomatoes, stock, oregano, bay leaf, and salt. Bring to a boil, reduce the heat to low, and simmer for 45 minutes, uncovered.

Stir in masa harina and mix well. Lumps will tend to appear at this point and should be broken up against the side of the pot with the back of a large serving spoon. Smaller lumps will break up as they cook. Simmer for 15 minutes. Stir in the black beans and the crabmeat. Heat for 15 to 20 minutes.

Top each serving with a dollop of sour cream.

NOTE: Masa harina is dehydrated corn dough that has been finely ground for making tortillas and tamales. Look for it in Latin markets and well-stocked supermarkets.

Crab and Asparagus Soup

Serves 6 to 8

This is the quintessential Chesapeake springtime soup, with first-of-the-season, Eastern Shore asparagus and the succulent meat of blue crabs.

1 1/2 pounds asparagus
4 cups Fish Stock (page 61) or clam juice
4 tablespoons butter
1/4 cup all-purpose flour
4 egg yolks
1 1/2 cups heavy (whipping) cream

1 pound backfin or special crab-meat, picked over for shells
Juice of 1 lemon
1 teaspoon salt
Ground white pepper to taste
Pinch of ground mace or freshly grated nutmeg

Cut off the tough bottom stems of the asparagus stalks and discard. Cut off the tips and, in a small saucepan, cook in boiling salted water to cover until barely tender, about 5 minutes. Drain and rinse under cold water. Put aside.

In a medium saucepan combine the remaining asparagus and the fish stock and bring to a boil. Reduce the heat, cover, and simmer until very tender, about 20 minutes. Transfer the asparagus and stock to a blender or food processor and purée until smooth. Set aside.

In a heavy-bottomed pot, melt the butter over medium heat. Whisk in the flour and cook, stirring constantly, for 2 to 3 minutes. Take care not to brown the flour.

Off the heat stir in the asparagus purée. Cook, stirring often, until thickened, about 15 minutes.

While the soup is cooking, combine the egg yolks and 1 cup of the cream in a large mixing bowl. Whisk until well mixed. Ladle out about one quarter of the soup and slowly whisk it into the yolk mixture. Turn the heat under the soup down to very low and slowly stir in the egg-cream mixture. Continue stirring until slightly thickened.

Add the crabmeat, reserved asparagus tips, and lemon juice. Simmer gently for several minutes. Do not let the soup come to a boil. Season with salt, pepper, and mace or nutmeg.

Lightly whip the remaining 1/2 cup cream. Serve the soup garnished with dollops of the cream.

Mama Lan's Blue Crab Curry

Serves 8 to 10

Mama Lan Huynh, a renowned Vietnamese chef and my "other mother," has probably prepared more Chesapeake fare than most Chesapeake homemakers. Mama has worked with me for many years in Berkeley, California, bringing Chesapeake delights to countless West Coast crab devotees. Here Mama brings a zesty Southeast Asian flair to our Chesapeake crab. Absolutely incredible, and so is Mama!

2 pounds backfin or claw crabmeat, picked over for shells
3/4 cup olive oil
1 tablespoon minced garlic
2 tablespoons fresh lemon juice
1/2 cup Madras curry powder
1 teaspoon salt
Freshly ground black pepper

Curry Sauce (recipe follows)
6 to 8 cups freshly steamed short- or medium-grain white rice
Condiments (small amounts of each): diced green bell pepper; diced red bell pepper; cored, seeded, and diced tomato; peeled and diced cucumber; peeled and diced carrot; diced pineapple; raisins; shredded, dried coconut

Place the crabmeat in a large bowl and set aside.

In a small bowl mix together 1/2 cup of the olive oil, garlic, lemon juice, curry powder, salt, and pepper. Pour the oil mixture over the crabmeat, toss well, and refrigerate for several hours.

About 45 minutes before you are ready to cook the curry, prepare the curry sauce, then put the rice on to cook.

In a heavy-bottomed pot, heat the remaining 1/4 cup olive oil over medium heat. Add the crab mixture and sauté gently for 2 minutes. Pour in the Curry Sauce and simmer over medium heat for 15 minutes.

Serve with the steamed rice and the condiments.

Let guests help themselves and add what they like to the curry.

Curry Sauce

3 tablespoons olive oil
2 small onions, finely diced
3 stalks fresh lemongrass, leafy tops discarded and bulb end finely diced
1 tablespoon minced garlic
3 tablespoons tomato paste
1/2 cup Madras curry powder
Two 14-ounce cans coconut milk

3 tablespoons sugar
12 tablespoons (1/4 pound plus 4 tablespoons) butter
1/2 cup cornstarch
3 1/4 cups water
1 2/3 cups heavy (whipping) cream
8 to 10 small red potatoes, peeled
Vegetable oil for deep-frying

In a heavy-bottomed pot, heat the olive oil over medium-high heat. Add the onions and lemongrass and sauté until the onions are golden brown, 6 to 8 minutes. Add the garlic, tomato paste, and curry powder. Cook for several minutes over medium heat, stirring often.

Off the heat stir in the coconut milk, sugar, and butter. Return to medium heat and stir until the butter is melted.

In a small bowl combine the cornstarch and about 1/2 cup of the water. Stir to form a thin, smooth paste, adding more water if needed. Stir the remaining 2 3/4 cups water, cornstarch mixture, and cream into the sauce. Cook over medium heat, stirring often, for 30 minutes.

While the sauce is cooking, pour the vegetable oil into a deep skillet or deep-fat fryer until it reaches a depth of about 3 inches and heat to 375°F. Slip the potatoes into the oil, a few at a time, and fry just until golden brown, about 5 to 6 minutes. Remove to paper towels to drain.

Strain the sauce through a fine sieve and discard the solids. Return the strained sauce to the pot and add the fried potatoes. Simmer until the potatoes are tender, about 30 minutes.

· Main Dishes ·

In Brooklyn, Maryland, along Route 2, a Harley-Davidson breezes
by a landmark crab painting on the side of a house.

Charm City Crab Imperial

Serves 4

This imperial wins my vote for some of the finest blue crab eating to be found on either side of the Bay. Imperials are richly spiced crab casseroles that are usually served in individual portions, either in the top shells of crabs or in ramekins. Each Chesapeake region, neighborhood, family, or restaurant, hoping to outdo one another, claims that its very own secret recipe is the absolute best, and the only one that truly impresses the imperial-jaded dinner guest.

6 tablespoons butter
1 small green bell pepper, seeded, deveined, and diced
1 small red bell pepper or pimiento, seeded, deveined, and finely diced
1/2 cup diced fresh mushrooms
3/4 cup mayonnaise
1 tablespoon Dijon-style mustard
1 tablespoon Worcestershire sauce

1/8 teaspoon Tabasco sauce
1/2 teaspoon Old Bay seasoning
1/2 teaspoon ground black pepper
1 teaspoon drained capers, chopped
Juice of 1/2 lemon
3 tablespoons chopped fresh parsley
1 pound lump or backfin crabmeat, picked over for shells
Imperial Topping (recipe follows)
Paprika for garnish

Preheat the oven to 350°F.

In a small skillet melt the butter over medium-high heat. Add the green and red bell peppers and mushrooms and sauté until soft, about 5 minutes. Put aside.

Combine the mayonnaise, mustard, Worcestershire sauce, Tabasco sauce, Old Bay, black pepper, capers, lemon juice, and parsley in a small bowl. Mix well. Add the sautéed peppers and mushrooms and stir in to combine thoroughly.

Place the crabmeat in a mixing bowl and pour the sautéed pepper mixture over the top. Toss gently, taking care not to break up the lumps of crabmeat. Spoon the mixture into a 1/2-quart casserole or into 4 individual scallop shells or well-cleaned crab top shells. Bake for 20 to 25 minutes.

While the imperial is baking, prepare the topping. When the imperial is done, remove from the oven and preheat the broiler. Spoon the topping evenly over the large or individual casseroles and sprinkle with paprika. Place under the broiler until nicely browned, 1 to 2 minutes. (If a broiler is unavailable, brown the top in the oven. It will take a bit longer.)

Serve immediately.

Imperial Topping

Makes about 1/3 cup

1 egg, beaten
1/4 cup mayonnaise

1 tablespoon chopped fresh parsley

In a small bowl combine the egg, mayonnaise, and parsley. Mix well.

Colonial Crabmeat Imperial

Serves 4

In Early American cooking, flour-based sauces were an indication of high social status. Refined white flour was quite expensive and not readily available. This recipe features a rich cream sauce base that is delightfully seasoned and very affordable.

3 tablespoons butter
2 tablespoons all-purpose flour
1 cup heavy (whipping) cream
1 egg, beaten
1/2 teaspoon dry mustard
1 teaspoon Worcestershire sauce
1/2 teaspoon salt
1/8 teaspoon cayenne pepper

2 tablespoons dry sherry
Dash of Tabasco sauce
2 tablespoons chopped fresh parsley
1 pound lump or backfin crabmeat, picked over for shells
Buttered fine dried bread crumbs for topping

Preheat the oven to 375°F.

In a small saucepan melt the butter over medium heat. Whisk in the flour and cook, stirring constantly, for 2 to 3 minutes. Do not let the flour brown. Slowly whisk in the cream and cook until quite smooth and thick, about 15 minutes.

Off the heat add all of the remaining ingredients, except the crabmeat, and mix well.

Place the crabmeat in a mixing bowl. Pour the cream mixture over the top. Toss gently, taking care not to break up the lumps of crabmeat. Butter a 6-cup casserole or baking dish and pour the crab mixture into it. Top with the bread crumbs and bake for 20 to 25 minutes or until nicely browned. Serve at once.

Mom Kimmel's "No Bell Pepper" Crabmeat Imperial

Serves 4

Mom Kimmel, down on Back River, is no fan of bell peppers or of jazzed-up seafood seasonings and she tells it like it is. "You ever see all those things they put in them fancy seafood seasonings?" she asks. "Only thing they left out is sand! And I'll never understand putting all

1 egg
1/2 cup mayonnaise
1 tablespoon dry mustard
1/2 teaspoon black pepper
1/4 teaspoon cayenne pepper

Pinch of salt
2 tablespoons chopped fresh parsley
1 pound backfin or lump crabmeat, picked over for shells
Paprika for garnish

Preheat the oven to 350°F.

In a small bowl combine the egg, mayonnaise, mustard, black pepper, cayenne pepper, salt, and parsley. Mix well.

Place the crabmeat in a large bowl and pour the batter over the top. Gently toss together, taking care not to break up the lumps of crabmeat.

*those bell peppers in imperial!
They're too potent and over-
power the taste of the crab."
Well, Mrs. Kimmel, after chat-
ting with a bushel and a peck of
Bay folk, I found you're not
alone. So, for all you out there
who aren't partial to bell peppers, here's one for you. Thanks,
Mom!*

Spoon the mixture into a 6-cup casserole dish or into well-scrubbed crab top shells. Lightly dust with paprika. Bake for 20 to 25 minutes.

Serve at once.

Heart-Smart Imperial Crab

Serves 4

*You've heard of the Chesapeake's
famous Lady Baltimore cake?
Well, now meet Lady Baltimore
herself, Eleanor Holliday Cross.
A Baltimore community leader,
actress, and avid traveler, Eleanor is also a zestful lover of life,
and spending an evening in her
company is enough to lift one's
spirit. Here Eleanor gives an
arterial-friendly yet delicious
recipe for those of us who enjoy
rich imperial crab but are looking to cut down on cholesterol.*

*3 tablespoons plus 4 teaspoons low-
 cholesterol mayonnaise*
1/2 teaspoon Worcestershire sauce
1/2 teaspoon Dijon-style mustard
*1 tablespoon minced green bell
 pepper*
1 tablespoon minced parsley
*1/4 cup liquid egg substitute
 (Scramblers or Eggbeaters)*

*1 scant teaspoon salt ("I use Jane's
 Crazy Mixed-up Salt")*
1/4 teaspoon ground white pepper
*1 pound backfin crabmeat, picked
 over for shells*
*1 heaping teaspoon no-cholesterol
 margarine, melted*
Paprika for garnish

Preheat the oven to 400°F.

In a small bowl combine the 3 tablespoons of mayonnaise, Worcester-shire sauce, mustard, bell pepper, parsley, egg substitute, salt, and pepper. Mix well.

Place the crabmeat in a large bowl and pour the mayonnaise mixture over the top. Toss gently, taking care not to break up the lumps of crabmeat.

Brush 4 scallop shells with the margarine and mound one-fourth of the crab mixture in each shell. Top each mound with 1 teaspoon of the remaining mayonnaise and dust lightly with paprika. Bake until nicely browned, about 20 minutes.

Serve at once.

*Eleanor Holliday Cross of Baltimore,
Maryland, is a remarkable woman—
always on the go. She is involved in
myriad civic, community, and artistic
endeavors, and cooking is one of her
great passions.*

Naunny's Crabmeat and Mushroom Linguine

Serves 6 to 8

Wanna know about food or what's going awry with today's generation? Just ask Mealy ("Naunny" to her scores of grandchildren and great grand-children) Sartori, and she'll tell you point-blank, "They're all crazy! Nobody wants to cook no more." But Mealy's still cooking and nobody does it better. Here's a dish to dazzle nostrils and taste buds alike. When she makes this crab pasta, the kids are always hanging around the sauce pot. "I tell 'em, don't you pick!" Then putting her hands up in mock exasperation she adds, "But they always do." So do yourself a favor. Whip up a batch of this pasta and let the picking begin.

1/2 cup olive oil
1 small onion, finely diced
3 large cloves garlic, minced
1/2 teaspoon hot-pepper flakes
One 6-ounce can tomato paste
One 28-ounce can crushed tomatoes
One 8-ounce can tomato sauce
2 cups water
1 teaspoon sugar
1 teaspoon salt

1/4 teaspoon ground black pepper
1/2 teaspoon dried oregano
1/2 teaspoon dried basil
1/2 pound small fresh mushrooms, trimmed and quartered
1 pound special or backfin crab-meat, picked over for shells
1 pound imported Italian linguine
Freshly grated Parmesan cheese and Italian bread for serving

In a heavy-bottomed saucepan, heat 1/4 cup of the olive oil over medium-high heat. Add the onion, garlic, and hot-pepper flakes and sauté until the onion turns a light golden brown, 6 to 8 minutes. Add the tomato paste and cook over medium-low heat, stirring frequently to prevent scorching, for 20 minutes.

Add the crushed tomatoes, tomato sauce, and water. Stir until smooth. Add the sugar, salt, pepper, oregano, and basil. Cover and simmer over very low heat for 1 hour.

While the sauce is cooking, heat the remaining 1/4 cup olive oil in a skillet over medium heat. Add the mushrooms and lightly sauté for about 3 minutes. Remove from the heat and set aside.

Stir the mushrooms and the crabmeat into the sauce. Cover and continue simmering over very low heat for 1 hour.

Following the manufacturer's instructions, cook the linguine in plenty of salted boiling water until just tender. Drain well in a colander. Place the linguine in a large pasta bowl and pour on just enough of the sauce to coat generously. Toss well.

Serve the remaining sauce in a bowl on the side. Pass around the Parmesan cheese and crusty bread.

Crabmeat Soufflé Norfolk

Serves 4

Memories of southern planta-
tions and gracious hospitality
come to mind when you bite into
this light and airy crabmeat
soufflé scented with bits of
Smithfield ham.

4 tablespoons butter
3 tablespoons plus 2/3 cup finely
  shredded Swiss cheese
1/3 cup finely diced Smithfield ham
2 tablespoons finely diced red bell
  pepper
2 tablespoons finely diced green bell
  pepper
3 tablespoons all-purpose flour
1 cup milk

2 tablespoons dry sherry
4 egg yolks
1/2 teaspoon salt
1/4 teaspoon ground black pepper
Freshly grated nutmeg
1/4 teaspoon Tabasco sauce
2 cups backfin or lump crabmeat
  (about 1 pound), picked over for
  shells
6 egg whites, stiffly beaten

Preheat the oven to 375°F. Butter a 2-quart soufflé dish and sprinkle the bottom of the dish with 3 tablespoons cheese.

In a heavy-bottomed enamelware pan, melt the butter over medium-high heat. Add the ham and the red and green bell peppers and sauté for several minutes until the peppers are soft. Whisk in the flour and cook, stirring constantly, for 2 to 3 minutes. Be careful not to brown the flour.

Off the heat slowly whisk in the milk and sherry. Return to medium heat and bring almost to a boil, stirring all the while. Off the heat beat in the egg yolks, one at a time. Season well with salt, pepper, and nutmeg. Stir in the Tabasco and the remaining 2/3 cup cheese. Lightly fold in the crabmeat, taking care not to break up the lumps of crab.

Beat the egg whites until stiff peaks form. Stir about one-fourth of the whites into the crab mixture to lighten it, then gently fold in the remaining whites. Pour the crab mixture into the prepared dish. Bake until nicely browned and firm, about 30 minutes.

Serve at once.

NOTE: For an interesting variation, add 1 teaspoon of Madras curry powder to the soufflé base with the nutmeg.

Deviled Crab

Serves 4 to 6

During the 1920s, this spicy crab casserole was all the culinary rage on the East Coast. Crab packers would always include the crab top shells with packed pounds of crabmeat so that the popular deviled dish could be served in them. Those days may be gone, but you still gotta give the devil his due!

4 tablespoons butter
2 tablespoons minced yellow onion
2 tablespoons minced green onion
2 tablespoons all-purpose flour
1 teaspoon dry mustard
1 teaspoon Dijon-style mustard
1 cup heavy (whipping) cream
1 teaspoon Worcestershire sauce
1 teaspoon salt
1/4 teaspoon ground white pepper
1/8 teaspoon cayenne pepper
Dash of Tabasco sauce
1 pound backfin crabmeat, picked over for shells
2 hard-cooked eggs, chopped
2 tablespoons chopped fresh parsley
Buttered fine dried bread crumbs for topping

Preheat the oven to 375°F. Butter a 6-cup baking dish and set aside. In a heavy-bottomed saucepan, melt the butter over medium-high heat. Add the yellow and green onions and sauté until soft, about 2 minutes. Whisk in the flour and dry mustard and cook for several minutes, stirring all the while.

Off the heat stir in the Dijon-style mustard, cream, Worcestershire sauce, salt, white pepper, cayenne pepper, and Tabasco sauce. Return to medium heat and cook, stirring often, until thickened, about 10 minutes.

Place the crabmeat, eggs, and parsley in a large mixing bowl. Pour the cream mixture over the top and toss gently. Pour into the prepared baking dish and top with the bread crumbs. Bake until nicely browned, 25 to 30 minutes.

Serve at once.

Crabmeat Pasticcio

Serves 6 to 8

Here's a robust Old World casserole from Baltimore's gastronomic team, Maria McMahan and Gus Pasquale. Maria emigrated to the Chesapeake from Greece and, along with the Italian Mr. Gus, has been wowing the Monumental City with their festive dinner parties. This is a perfect, easy-to-prepare dish for

1 pound ziti (large pasta tubes)
Two 10 3/4-ounce cans cream of shrimp soup, undiluted
1 pound backfin or lump crabmeat, picked over for shells
4 tablespoons butter
1/4 cup all-purpose flour
2 cups milk, heated
2 eggs, beaten

Preheat the oven to 375°F. Butter a 9-by-13-inch baking dish.

Following the manufacturer's instructions, cook the ziti in boiling salted water until just tender. Drain well in a colander and set aside in a large mixing bowl. Meanwhile, in a saucepan over medium heat, combine the cream of shrimp soup and the crabmeat and heat gently until hot. Pour the crabmeat mixture over the ziti and fold together gently, taking care not to

a large gathering. Maria adds, *"It'sa delish . . . and would I a-steer-a yoo wrong?"* Serve with a tossed garden salad and plenty of crusty Italian bread.

break up the lumps of crabmeat. Pour into the prepared baking dish and set aside.

In a heavy-bottomed saucepan, melt the butter over medium heat. Whisk in the flour and cook, stirring constantly, for 2 to 3 minutes. Take care not to brown the flour.

Off the heat slowly whisk in the milk. Then whisk in the eggs, one at a time, and return to low heat. Cook, stirring all the while, until the mixture is the consistency of a light custard, about 15 minutes.

Pour the milk mixture evenly over the pasta mixture. Bake until set, about 30 minutes.

Stuffed Sole Fillets Meunière

Serves 6

In this recipe delicate fillets of sole are wrapped around mounds of imperial, wine baked, and then topped with a lovely lemon butter. The dish forms the centerpiece for an exquisite Chesapeake dining experience. Serve with a saffron-infused rice (see Note) and tender asparagus tips.

1 batch of your favorite crabmeat imperial (page 69 to 71)
Six 6-ounce sole fillets, or twelve 3-ounce sole fillets
About 2 tablespoons melted butter
Salt and ground black pepper to taste for cooking fillets

1/4 cup fresh lemon juice
2 cups dry white wine
1/2 teaspoon freshly ground white pepper
1/4 cup chopped fresh parsley

Preheat the oven to 375°F. Prepare the imperial and put aside.

Place the sole fillets, skin side up, on a flat work surface. Spread each fillet with some of the imperial mixture and roll up into a cylinder. Arrange seam side down in a glass baking dish in which they fit without crowding. Brush the tops of the rolled fillets with butter. Sprinkle lightly with salt, pepper, and lemon juice. Pour the wine around the fillets and cover the baking dish with aluminum foil. Bake for 20 to 25 minutes.

Remove the fillets with a slotted utensil to a heated platter; keep warm while making the sauce. Strain the cooking juices into a saucepan and place over high heat. Boil until reduced to 3 tablespoons.

In a small, heavy-bottomed saucepan, melt the butter over low heat until it turns a light reddish brown. Remove from the heat and add the lemon juice, 1/2 teaspoon pepper, reduced pan juices, and parsley. Whisk to blend and return to the heat for about 1 minute.

Spoon the hot sauce over the fillets and serve at once.

NOTE: To make a saffron-flavored rice, simply add a touch of powdered Spanish saffron to your rice water.

Rockfish with Crabmeat Hollandaise

Serves 4

For a number of years, there was a fishing ban on the Chesapeake's most famous fin fish, the rock. Limited commercial fishing has been allowed to resume, however, and those who have never experienced rockfish are in for quite the treat. And topped with lightly sautéed lumps of crabmeat and hollandaise . . . well, what can I say except "seafood ecstasy."

Loretta Larrimore aboard the skipjack, The Lady Katie, at dock at the family's home in Fairbank, Tilghman Island. When she and her husband, Captain Stanley Larrimore, ran summmer charters for guests on The Ladie Katie, Loretta did the on-board food preparation and was renowned for her Chesapeake dinners. They had many repeat customers, some of whom are still calling.

Hollandaise Sauce (page 36)
8 tablespoons (1/4 pound) butter
1 pound backfin crabmeat, picked over for shells
1/4 cup minced fresh chives

2 tablespoons fresh lemon juice
Salt and ground white pepper
Four 6- to 8-ounce rockfish fillets (cod, snapper, or flounder may be substituted)

Preheat the broiler. Prepare the sauce and keep warm.

In a sauté pan melt 4 tablespoons of the butter over medium heat. Add the crabmeat and chives and sauté gently until heated through, 3 to 5 minutes. Take care not to break up the lumps of crabmeat. Hold in a warm oven.

In a small pan over medium heat, melt the remaining 4 tablespoons butter. Stir in the lemon juice and a little salt and pepper. Coat a broiler pan with some of the melted butter. Place the fillets on the pan, skin side down, and brush with the remaining melted butter.

Broil about 4 inches from the flame until just cooked through, 4 to 6 minutes.

Serve the fillets on heated plates with the crabmeat mounded down the center of each fillet. Top each serving with the warm sauce.

Rockfish Stuffed with Crabmeat

Serves 4 or 5

This is a truly classic Chesapeake preparation for the fabled rock-fish. It's pure, simple, and delicious. If rockfish is not available, you may substitute other whole fish such as black bass, trout, or sea trout.

One 3- to 4-pound rockfish, cleaned
8 tablespoons butter
Juice of 1 lemon
1 pound backfin or special crab-meat, picked over for shells
Salt and ground black pepper to taste
4 strips bacon
1 cup milk

Preheat the oven to 350°F. With a sharp boning knife, make a shallow cut along the belly of the fish where it has already been cut for gutting. This will create a pocket.

In a small pan melt the butter over medium heat. Stir in the lemon juice. Place the crabmeat in a mixing bowl and pour the melted butter over the top. Toss gently, taking care not to break up the lumps of crabmeat. Stuff the crab mixture inside the fish.

Place the fish in a glass baking dish and sprinkle with salt and pepper. Arrange the strips of bacon over the fish. Pour the milk into the bottom of the baking dish.

Bake until the fish flakes at the touch of a fork, 50 minutes to 1 hour. If toward the end of the baking the bacon is turning too brown, cover the dish loosely with aluminum foil.

Serve at once.

Shrimp Stuffed with Crabmeat
à la Dolores

Serves 4 or 5

You can tell by the aroma pulling you up the steps of Dolores Keh's row house in Baltimore's Little Italy that there's some good cooking going on inside. Her hearty, infectious laughter lights up the kitchen, as she keeps setting delicious platter after delicious platter in front of her guests. Not only is Dolores a wizard in the kitchen, but she married one as well. Her husband Rolando is a chef for the United States Congress in Washington, D.C. It's a food family! Dolores suggests serving these wonderful stuffed shrimp with a tangy cocktail sauce, macaroni and cheese, steamed broccoli, and corn bread. After all that good eating it'll be hard to tell who's stuffed, the shrimp or you!

Baltimore native Delores Keh, one of Little Italy's finest cooks and all around good-time gal, prepares a bowl of succulent crabs. Dolores loves cooking and loves feeding people even more. No one has ever been known to leave her house hungry and to this I can attest!

Cocktail Sauce (recipe follows)
1 pound jumbo shrimp
1 egg
2 heaping tablespoons mayonnaise
1 teaspoon prepared mustard
1/4 cup Old Bay seasoning
1 teaspoon Worcestershire sauce
1/4 cup chopped fresh parsley
2 slices white bread, diced and soaked in milk just to cover
1 pound backfin crabmeat, picked over for shells

Coating
1 cup flour seasoned with salt and ground black pepper
3 eggs, beaten
1 cup or so fine dried bread crumbs

Vegetable oil for frying
Lemon wedges

Prepare the sauce and set aside.

Peel the shrimp, leaving on the last ring of shell and the tail. Devein and then butterfly along the inside curve of the body. Set aside.

In a small bowl combine the egg, mayonnaise, mustard, Old Bay, Worcestershire sauce, and parsley. Mix well.

Place the crabmeat and soaked bread in a large mixing bowl and pour the egg mixture over the top. Toss gently, taking care not to break up the lumps of crabmeat.

Arrange the shrimp on a baking sheet or platter, flattening the bodies. Firmly mound some of the crab mixture on each shrimp.

To coat the shrimp, first dust them with the seasoned flour, then dip them in the beaten egg, and, lastly, lightly coat them with the bread crumbs.

In a large skillet pour in vegetable oil to a depth of 1 inch or so and heat over medium-high heat. Add the shrimp and fry, turning occasionally, until golden brown, about 3 to 5 minutes. Remove to paper towels to drain briefly.

Serve at once with the lemon wedges and sauce.

Cocktail Sauce

Makes about 2 1/2 cups

2 cups ketchup
1/2 cup prepared horseradish
2 tablespoons Worcestershire sauce

1/2 teaspoon Tabasco sauce
Juice of 1 lemon

In a small bowl combine all of the ingredients. Mix well.

Estelle's Blue Crabs and Spaghetti

Serves 6 to 8

During the Great Depression you needed to stretch things to get by, and in those days both tomatoes and crabs were cheap. Not anymore, of course. So Estelle DiMarino of Carney, Maryland, who is a crab cooker from way back, only prepares this, her delicious finger-licking signature dish, for special occasions.

2 tablespoons olive oil
12 live male blue crabs, cleaned
  and halved (page 11)
8 ripe fresh tomatoes, cored, peeled,
  seeded, and chopped
One 12-ounce can tomato paste
One 12-ounce can tomato sauce

2 cloves garlic, minced
1 tablespoon chopped fresh basil
1 teaspoon dried oregano
Salt and ground black pepper to
  taste
2 cups water
1 pound spaghetti

In a large, heavy-bottomed pot, heat the olive oil over medium-high heat. Add the crabs and sauté, turning often, for 6 to 8 minutes. Add all of the remaining ingredients, except the spaghetti. Cover and simmer over low heat for about 2 hours.

Following the manufacturer's instructions, cook the spaghetti in plenty of salted boiling water until just tender. Drain well in a colander and then turn into a large pasta bowl. Pour about half of the sauce over the spaghetti and toss to coat the noodles. Arrange the crabs on top of the pasta. Serve the remaining sauce in a bowl on the side. Don't forget to have plenty of napkins on hand. It may be necessary to hose down the children after the meal.

Crabmeat Étouffée with Waffles

Serves 4

Louisiana is the home of this classic dish, which is traditionally served over rice. Étouffée means "smothered in," and here crabmeat is smothered in a zesty mélange of vegetables and fish broth. This rendition has the crabmeat bathed in an aromatic Cajun "gravy" of étouffée juices and then mounded atop light waffles, which are a delightful departure from the usual steamed rice.

6 tablespoons butter
1/4 cup all-purpose flour
2 tablespoons minced garlic
1 cup finely chopped yellow onion
1/2 cup finely chopped green onion
1/2 cup finely chopped celery
1 small green bell pepper, seeded, deveined, and finely diced
1 teaspoon salt
1/4 teaspoon ground black pepper
1/4 teaspoon cayenne pepper
1/4 teaspoon Tabasco sauce
Juice of 1 lemon
3 cups Fish Stock (page 61)
1/4 cup chopped fresh parsley
1 pound special or claw crabmeat, picked over for shells
Waffles (recipe follows)

In a heavy-bottomed pot, melt the butter over medium-high heat. Whisk in the flour and cook, stirring constantly, until the roux turns a dark reddish brown color, about 5 to 8 minutes. Keep it moving or it'll burn!

Off the heat stir in the garlic, yellow and green onions, celery, and bell pepper. Return to the heat and cook, stirring frequently, until the vegetables are tender, about 20 minutes.

Add the salt, black pepper, cayenne pepper, Tabasco sauce, and lemon juice. Stir in the fish stock, mixing well. Bring to a boil, reduce the heat to

When Mildred Ripley moved to Baltimore years ago and was about to learn the art of crab picking, her friend Mike Delea designed this suit to help her through her early attempts. Now she no longer needs the suit as she has become quite proficient at taking a crab apart. Here she models her now-retired garb as her sister, Mary Dills, sips a beer in the background.

low, and simmer covered for 30 to 45 minutes. Stir in the parsley and crabmeat and continue simmering uncovered for 30 minutes.

While the étouffée is cooking, prepare the waffles. Arrange the waffles on warmed plates and spoon the étouffée over the top.

Waffles

Makes 4 waffles

1 cup all-purpose flour
2 teaspoons baking powder
1/4 teaspoon salt
2 teaspoons sugar

3/4 cup milk
1 egg, beaten
1 1/2 tablespoons butter, melted
and cooled

Preheat the waffle iron. In a mixing bowl sift together the flour, baking powder, salt, and sugar. In a second bowl mix together the milk, egg, and butter. Gradually add the wet ingredients to the dry, stirring until thoroughly combined.

Following the manufacturer's instructions, cook the batter in the waffle iron until golden brown.

Crabmeat and Shrimp Jambalaya

Serves 6 to 8

Here's more cooking from the bayou. The "razapee" comes from Mr. Jackie Lee, who packed his bags down in his native Louisiana after World War II and headed north to Baltimore in search of a factory job. He may have left the home of his youth far behind, but he did bring with him a well-worn cooking pot in which he brews up some of the finest Cajun treats you've ever put your lips to.

3 tablespoons bacon drippings or vegetable oil
1/4 pound tasso (Cajun-style smoked pork butt), finely diced
1/4 pound andouille Cajun pork sausage, finely diced
2 cups diced onion
1 cup diced celery
1 cup diced green bell pepper
2 tablespoons minced garlic
1/4 cup chopped fresh parsley
1 tablespoon salt
1/2 teaspoon ground white pepper
1/4 teaspoon cayenne pepper
2 bay leaves

1/2 teaspoon dried thyme
1/4 teaspoon dried oregano
1/4 teaspoon dried basil
1/8 teaspoon ground cloves
1/8 teaspoon ground mace
4 cups chopped fresh or canned tomatoes
2 cups Fish Stock (page 61) or water
2 cups long-grain white rice
1 pound claw or special crabmeat, picked over for shells
1 pound medium shrimp, peeled and deveined

In a large, heavy-bottomed soup pot, heat the bacon drippings or oil over high heat. Add the tasso and andouille and sauté for 3 to 5 minutes. Add the onion, celery, bell pepper, and garlic. Cook, stirring frequently, until the vegetables are tender, about 15 minutes.

Stir in the parsley, salt, white pepper, cayenne pepper, bay leaves, thyme, oregano, basil, cloves, and mace. Mix well. Add the tomatoes and stock or water. Bring to a boil, reduce the heat to low, and simmer for 15 minutes.

Add the rice and bring back to a boil. Cover, reduce the heat to very low, and cook for 20 minutes. Stir in the crabmeat and shrimp, re-cover, and continue simmering for 25 minutes. Now and then remove the cover and give the pot a stir so that the rice does not stick. During the last 10 minutes of cooking, remove the cover, increase the heat a bit, and stir often to dry out the rice.

Serve at once.

Crabmeat and Shrimp Pot Pie

Serves 8

As you may have noticed, those crab and shrimp seem to travel in packs. Here's another arranged marriage of these tasty shellfish, potted, so to speak, in an all-American savory pie. They swim in a mornay-style sauce and are topped by a delicate flaky pastry topping. You can also make individual-sized pies. If you make more than needed, they freeze nicely, too. Simply cool to room temperature, top the assembled pot pies with pastry, wrap tightly in plastic wrap, and freeze until ready to use.

Flaky Pastry (recipe follows)
Pot Pie Sauce (recipe follows)
4 tablespoons butter
1 clove garlic, minced
1 pound shrimp, peeled, deveined, and cut into 1-inch pieces
1 pound backfin or special crabmeat, picked over for shells
1/2 pound small fresh mushrooms, cut into quarters

2 ripe fresh tomatoes, peeled, seeded, and chopped
1/4 cup chopped fresh basil
Salt and freshly ground black pepper
1/4 cup freshly grated Parmesan or Asiago cheese
1 egg yolk
2 tablespoons cold water

Prepare the pastry and refrigerate. Prepare the pie sauce and set aside while putting together the casserole. Preheat the oven to 375°F. Butter a 14-by-8-by-2-inch baking dish or other 2-quart casserole.

In a skillet melt the butter over medium-high heat. Add the garlic and lightly sauté without browning, 1 to 2 minutes. Add the shrimp, crabmeat, and mushrooms. Cook over medium heat for 3 minutes. Add the tomatoes and basil and mix well. Season lightly with salt and pepper. Remove from the heat and combine with the sauce, mixing well.

Pour the seafood mixture into the prepared baking dish. Sprinkle the cheese evenly over top.

On a lightly floured board, roll out the pastry dough into a rectangle large enough to fit the top of the baking dish or casserole. Lay the pastry over the top of the dish, trim off the excess, and flute the edges against the dish rim.

In a small bowl beat together the egg yolk and water and brush the top of the pastry. With a sharp knife, make several small slits in the pastry to allow steam to escape. Bake until the crust is golden brown, 25 to 30 minutes.

Serve at once.

Flaky Pastry

Makes enough pastry to top 1 large pot pie or 4 to 6 individual pies

2 1/4 cups all-purpose flour
1 teaspoon salt

3/4 cup solid vegetable shortening
5 to 7 tablespoons ice water

Sift together the flour and salt into a mixing bowl. Using your fingertips or a pastry blender, work the shortening into the flour until the mixture is the consistency of coarse meal.

Add the water, 1 tablespoon at a time, and mix with a fork after each addition. The dough should not be wet, but just moist enough to hold together. Form the dough into a ball. Wrap in plastic wrap and refrigerate for at least 15 minutes or for up to 1 hour before rolling out. This is the source of the expression "get the ball rolling."

Pot Pie Sauce

Makes about 3 1/2 cups

5 tablespoons butter
5 tablespoons all-purpose flour
1 1/2 cups Fish Stock (page 61)
3 cups heavy (whipping) cream
1 cup freshly grated Parmesan or
   Asiago cheese

Salt and freshly ground black
   pepper
Freshly grated nutmeg

In a heavy-bottomed saucepan, melt the butter over medium heat. Whisk in the flour and cook, stirring constantly, for 2 to 3 minutes. Be careful not to brown the flour.

Off the heat slowly whisk in the stock and cream. Return to medium heat and heat, stirring constantly, until the sauce reaches a boil.

Remove from the heat and gradually stir in the cheese. Season well with salt, pepper, and nutmeg.

Bessie's Crab Puddin'

Serves 6

My great-aunt Bessie, Gawd love her, was a southern spinster lady who did not spend a great deal of time in the kitchen. Fact of the matter is, she made only two things, chow mein and her crab puddin'. Back then, the family was never big on chow mein. A bit too esoteric I suppose. But you couldn't keep them away from the table when they knew

6 tablespoons butter or bacon
   drippings
1/4 cup minced onion
1/2 cup finely diced celery
1 cup chopped fresh mushrooms
1/2 cup finely diced green bell
   pepper
1 pound backfin crabmeat, picked
   over for shells
8 slices white bread, crusts discarded and diced

4 eggs, lightly beaten
2 cups milk
2 cups heavy (whipping) cream
1 teaspoon salt
1/2 teaspoon ground black pepper
1 teaspoon Worcestershire sauce
Dash of Tabasco sauce
1 cup finely shredded sharp
   Cheddar cheese

Butter a 6-cup casserole or baking dish.

In a skillet melt the butter or bacon drippings over medium-high heat.

Bessie was baking up a pan of her savory crab pudding. This creamy casserole not only makes a fine dinner entrée but is also a good change of pace dish for a Sunday brunch. Serve with vine-ripened summer tomatoes and hot biscuits.

Add the onion, celery, mushrooms, and bell pepper and sauté until tender, about 5 minutes. Remove from the heat, fold in the crabmeat, and set aside.

Place half of the diced bread in the bottom of the prepared dish. Spread the crabmeat-vegetable mixture over the top. Place the remaining diced bread on top of the crab mixture.

In a mixing bowl combine the eggs, milk, cream, salt, pepper, Worcestershire sauce, and Tabasco sauce. Mix well and pour over the casserole. Cover with aluminum foil and "tuck it in the Frigidaire for a few hours, so it'll set up on ya."

Preheat the oven to 350°F. Just before baking, remove the foil and sprinkle the casserole with the cheese. Place in the oven and bake for 15 minutes. Reduce the heat to 325°F and continue baking until set, about 45 minutes. Serve hot.

In Solomons, Maryland, a souvenir stick-up crab at the Calvert Marina gift shop seems to hover over the Drum Point Lighthouse on the Museum's grounds.

Michael Paul's Fish Sticks

Serves 6 to 8

Not many fellows round the Chesapeake Bay know more about what the fish are thinking or where they're hiding than Michael Paul Dahl. He lives with his family on the banks of Middle River, Maryland, and likes nothing better than spending a day on the water trying to lure the fishies to his carefully baited hook. This recipe came to him while he was fishing blue gills around Denton, Maryland. The locals there were catching crabs, and, at the end of the day, between them and Michael, they had a pile of crabs and blue gills. Normally that would be an unlikely pairing, but Michael set his head to working and he crafted this absolutely scrumptious dish that makes Friday nights (or any other, for that matter) worth waiting for.

1 egg
1 heaping tablespoon mayonnaise
1 tablespoon dry mustard
1/2 teaspoon salt
1/2 teaspoon ground black pepper
1/4 teaspoon cayenne pepper
1 teaspoon dried tarragon
3 tablespoons chopped fresh parsley
1 pound backfin or claw crabmeat, picked over for shells

1 1/2 pounds fish fillets (blue gill, crappie, or any small whitefish fillets), cut into 3-by-1-inch pieces
2 cups Bisquick
1 3/4 cups ice water
Vegetable oil for frying
Lemon wedges

In a small bowl combine the egg, mayonnaise, mustard, salt, black pepper, cayenne pepper, tarragon, and parsley. Mix well.

Place the crabmeat in a large mixing bowl and pour the egg mixture over the top. Mix gently, taking care not to break up the lumps of crabmeat.

Line a baking sheet with waxed paper. Arrange the fish fillets on the baking sheet. Mound some of the crab mixture evenly on top of each fillet. It should be about 1/4 inch high. Place the baking sheet in the freezer until the fish and crab mixture is stiff, about 45 minutes.

Make a thin tempuralike batter out of the Bisquick and ice water. In a skillet pour in oil until it reaches a depth of about 1 inch and heat to 375°F. Being careful not to crowd the pan, dip each fillet into the batter, coating completely, and slip it into the pan, crabside down. Panfry turning once, until golden brown, 2 to 3 minutes on each side. Remove the fillets to paper towels to drain. If all the fillets do not fit in the skillet at once, hold the cooked fillets in a warm oven while the others are being fried.

Serve hot with plenty of lemon wedges.

Soft-shell crabs are featured at a market on Tilghman Island, an Eastern Shore watermen's community that has long been known as one of the Chesapeake's leading seafood centers.

Miss Alice's Crab Royale

Serves 6

Here we have another wonderful Eastern Shore bit of crab cookery from the Harrison family on the Tilghman Peninsula. This delicious dish is quick and easy to prepare and can be used as either an entrée or a dip.

4 tablespoons butter
4 medium-sized fresh mushrooms, sliced
1 cup heavy (whipping) cream
2 tablespoons brandy or sherry
2 tablespoons chopped fresh parsley

1/2 teaspoon salt
1/4 teaspoon ground black pepper
1 pound backfin crabmeat, picked over for shells
Toast points for garnish

In a sauté pan melt the butter over medium-high heat. Add the mushrooms and sauté until tender, 3 to 5 minutes. Add the cream, brandy, parsley, salt, pepper, and crabmeat. Cook gently until heated through.
Serve at once in warmed ramekins. Garnish with toast points.

Crabmeat au Gratin

Serves 6

There's a love affair going on between crabmeat and cheese right here in this casserole. Au gratin dishes are a cornerstone of Chesapeake cuisine, and this tasty recipe justifies that status.

4 tablespoons butter
1/4 cup all-purpose flour
1 cup heavy (whipping) cream
1 cup milk
1 teaspoon Worcestershire sauce
1/2 teaspoon salt
1/4 teaspoon ground black pepper

2 tablespoons finely diced celery
1 tablespoon grated onion
1 tablespoon chopped pimiento
3/4 cup shredded sharp Cheddar cheese
1 pound lump crabmeat, picked over for shells

Preheat the oven to 350°F. Butter a 6-cup casserole.

In a saucepan melt the butter over medium heat. Whisk in the flour and cook, stirring constantly, for 2 to 3 minutes. Be careful not to brown the flour.

Off the heat slowly whisk in the cream and milk. Stir in the Worcestershire sauce, salt, pepper, celery, onion, and pimiento. Add 1/2 cup of the cheese and the crabmeat and mix well.

Pour the mixture into the prepared casserole and top with the remaining 1/4 cup cheese. Bake until the cheese is lightly browned, about 20 minutes. Serve at once.

Medallions of Veal with Crabmeat and Mushrooms

Serves 6

Very few crab recipes feature such a remarkable complementary pairing, a fancy "surf and turf" if you will, of tender veal medallions and lumps of crabmeat. It's quite the extravagant dish, but when you want to pull out all the stops, this is the meal to choose. A four-star, putting-on-the-Ritz meal. A good accompaniment would be a cheese-laden polenta and steamed summer squash with lemon butter.

12 tablespoons butter
3/4 pound small fresh mushrooms, quartered
Salt and freshly ground black pepper to taste
2 tablespoons olive oil
Twelve 3-ounce veal medallions cut from tenderloin, pounded to 1/8 inch thick

1/2 cup dry Marsala wine
3 tablespoons concentrated veal stock or rich beef bouillon
1/4 cup chopped fresh parsley
1/4 cup minced fresh chives
1 pound backfin or lump crabmeat, picked over for shells

In a sauté pan melt 4 tablespoons of the butter over medium-high heat. Add the mushrooms and sauté until tender, about 5 minutes. Season with salt and pepper and set aside.

In a heavy skillet heat the olive oil and 2 tablespoons of the butter over medium-high heat. Add the veal medallions and sauté, turning several times, until cooked, about 2 minutes on each side. Remove the medallions and set aside; keep warm.

Pour off the oil and butter from the pan and pour in the Marsala. Cook over high heat, scraping up all browned bits, for 1 minute. Pour in the stock or bouillon and bring to a boil. Reduce the heat to low and slowly whisk in the remaining 6 tablespoons of butter, bit by bit. Season to taste with salt and pepper.

Dip each medallion in the sauce, coating well, and place on a warmed serving platter.

Gently fold the cooked mushrooms, parsley, chives, and crabmeat into the sauce, taking care not to break up the lumps of crabmeat. Heat gently.

Spoon the crabmeat sauce over the veal medallions.

"How much do you love me?" "A bushel and a peck!" In Chesapeake terms, that's a lot. Growing up, I remember everything being measured in bushels and pecks. The crabs are still packed and sold in bushel baskets along the Chesapeake. Here's a stack with their lids resting on a pier in Crisfield, Maryland.

Mediterranean-Style Grilled Blue Crabs

Serves 3 or 4

In the seafood cafés of Greece during the summer months, one finds grilled crabs smaller than Chesapeake blues. My Greek-Chesapeake cooking expert, Maria, tried a similar, pardon the expression, "execution," on the blue crab of the Chesapeake with outstanding results. This is a great idea for a Greek theme cookout that could also include a hearty feta cheese and kalamata olive salad, loaves of crusty bread, and chilled bottles of retsina.

12 live large male blue crabs
  (number 1 grade jimmies)

1 1/2 cups olive oil
Juice of 3 lemons

Light a fire in a charcoal grill.

In a steamer pot or large heavy pot with a tight-fitting lid, pour in water to a depth of 2 to 3 inches. Put a round raised rack into the pot that is tall enough to clear the liquid. Bring to a good strong boil.

Place the crabs on the rack, cover, and steam over moderately high heat until half cooked, 3 to 4 minutes. Remove the crabs from the rack and cool slightly.

With a sharp chef's knife, cut the body down the middle lengthwise, right through the shell, resulting in two halves with legs. Pull off the top shell and discard. Clean out the gills and the "devil" (see page 11).

In a small bowl mix together the olive oil and lemon juice. Pour off 1/3 cup of the mixture into a separate container to be used for basting the crabs.

Brush the crabs with the basting mixture and place on the hot grill. Cook, turning frequently, until the shells are bright red and the meat has turned from opaque to white.

Serve with the reserved oil-lemon mixture for dipping the meat.

Mama Lan's Vietnamese Stir-Fried Crabs

Serves 4

Dining on these stir-fried blue crabs is like taking a trip half-way around the world. Mama Lan is an expert with seafood cookery, and this exotic dish is almost as exciting to make as it is to eat. Serve these spicy crabs with bowls of steamed jasmine rice.

12 live large male blue crabs, cleaned and halved, with top shells reserved (page 00)
2 cups all-purpose flour seasoned with salt and ground black pepper
Vegetable oil for frying
6 tablespoons butter
6 tablespoons olive oil
3 stalks fresh lemongrass, grassy tops discarded and bulbs finely chopped

4 tablespoons minced garlic
3 tablespoons hot-pepper flakes
3 tablespoons kosher salt
3 tablespoons sugar
3-inch-piece fresh ginger root, peeled and julienned
1 bunch green onions, finely chopped
4 or 5 fresh serrano chiles, thinly sliced into rounds

Dredge the crabs in the seasoned flour. In a large skillet, pour in vegetable oil until it reaches a depth of 1/2 inch. Add the top shells and fry, turning, until crispy on both sides. Remove to paper towels to drain. Add the crab pieces, and fry over fairly high heat, turning frequently, until bright red, 5 to 7 minutes. Remove to paper towels to drain. Discard the cooking oil.

Place the pan back on medium heat and add the butter and olive oil. When the butter melts, add the lemongrass, garlic, and pepper flakes and sauté for about 30 seconds. Add the crab pieces (not the top shells) and sprinkle with the salt and sugar. Stir well. Add the ginger, green onions, and serrano chiles. Cook, stirring often, for 3 to 4 minutes.

Place the crab tops, hollow side up, on a platter. Tuck the crab pieces in the shells. Pour all of the pan juices over the stuffed shells. Serve at once, with plenty of napkins for messy hands.

Blue Crab Susoise

Serves 8

Our talented Chesapeake-born-and-bred chef Madame Susoise Gunn shows off her sautéing skills with this mouth-watering lump crabmeat dish. She adds that this recipe is good over pasta or rice or spooned into puff-pastry shells and also makes a great appetizer or hot crab dip. Way to go, Susoise!

2 tablespoons olive oil
1 teaspoon minced onion
1 teaspoon minced garlic
1 teaspoon freshly grated lemon peel
Juice of 1 lemon
1/2 cup sliced toasted almonds

1/2 cup dry white wine
2 cups heavy (whipping) cream
2 pounds lump crabmeat, picked over for shells
Salt and ground black pepper to taste

In a sauté pan heat the olive oil over medium-high heat. Add the onion and garlic and sauté for 1 to 2 minutes, taking care not to brown them. Add the lemon peel and juice, almonds, and wine. Bring to a full boil for 1 minute. Add the cream, bring to a boil, and reduce by one half.

Reduce the heat to low and add the crabmeat, tossing gently. Heat gently for 2 minutes. Season with salt and pepper.

Serve at once.

· References ·

Having trouble finding some Chesapeake foods at your local markets? Not to worry! Here are a few of the many Chesapeake fish mongers and distributors who will give flight to your crabs and crab accompaniments and have them winging their way to your doorstep in a matter of hours.

Old Bay Seasoning
P.O. Box 1802
Baltimore, Maryland   21203
1-800-632-5847

Faidley's Seafood
Lexington Market
200 N. Paca Street
Baltimore, Maryland   21202
(410)727-4898

Air-freighted crabmeat, crab cakes, steamed crabs, and seafood soups and gumbos, plus an array of fresh, in-season Chesapeake seafood.

Hale's Seafood
1801 Taylor Avenue
Baltimore, Maryland   21234
(410)665-4000

Air-freighted crabmeat, steamed crabs, crab cakes, and a wide variety of local seafood.

John T. Handy Company
P.O. Box 309
Crisfield, Maryland   21817
1-800-426-3977

Air-freighted soft-shell crabs of all shapes and sizes.

Nick's Inner Harbor Seafood
Cross Street Market
Baltimore, Maryland   21230
(410)685-2020

Air-freighted steamed crabs, crab cakes, and soft-shells, plus a tremendous assortment of locally caught shellfish and fish.

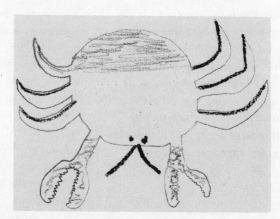

Martin Lotz
Kingsville Elementary School
Grade 5
Kingsville, Maryland

· Index ·